Casanova + Hernandez *Scale & Perception*

Casanova + Hernandez *Scale & Perception*

With images by Christian Richters

Wasmuth

Editor Ulrich Müller

Foreword

Ulrich Müller

Though the complexity of architecture ultimately can only be communicated in reality, architecture exhibitions are an important instrument for many architects in order to present their buildings and projects to the public. Even new media—which within the last ten years has revealed thus unimaginable possibilities for communication—has not changed that. The expanded palette of tools has, at most, contributed to the democratization of tools, if you will, for public debate about architecture. Whereas only a few years ago only big architecture offices had access to these means, the majority of architects today have access to the entire spectrum of essential communication tools. Nevertheless, it seems that the conventional and complex format of the exhibition has an inherently unique quality that rises above the advantages of new technological methods.

The potential of an exhibition lies not only in the transportation of architectural ideas to other places, in presenting them to a public that will not visit the real, constructed objects. In many cases, architects use the communication format of an exhibition for theoretical exercises that reach far beyond daily office life. The basis of this approach stems from the fact that one cannot simply simulate the experience of architecture in an exhibition space. Since essential characteristics of architecture, like space, body and surface cannot be copied or scaled down without drastically restricting their effect, inevitably new ideas must be developed. Successful exhibitions are not limited by the inadequacies of this transformation process, but rather recognize them as creative potential. Instead of the classical presentation of plans, for example, strategies are implemented whose origin often come from the arts. In art, communicating ideas through atmospheric density and representing functional carriers of meaning has more than just a broad and successfully tested tradition. The strategy of translation and interpretation is much more system immanent, since art functions exclusively through interpreted illustrations of reality. In the case of architecture exhibitions as well, the strategy depends on translating conditions and facts in such a way that the observer develops specific associations. The communication of an idea often plays a larger role than the presentation of actual dimensions, materials etc.

In the best case, installations emerge that are independent works. They serve not only as representatives of something real and existing, but rather show more than a real building is even capable of doing: With their expanded potential the architecture exhibition permits an intimate glimpse behind the scenes of architecture production and supports direct dialogue between designer and architectural consumer. For the architects, exhibitions become testing grounds for their thought processes; something promoted even further by the fact that an exhibition is not only visited by professionals, but by laypeople as well. Therefore the exhibition must also function on very different cultural levels.

Helena Casanova and Jesus Hernandez made good use of this knowledge and developed a strongly pictorial strategy for their exhibition. Titled *Scale & Perception*, they concentrate their translation in a minimalist installation, composed of two miniature walk-in spaces: One is a rectangular space, open on one side so that visitors can step inside, and made of plastic foil imprinted with a ginkgo-leaf motif; the other is a wood object, black outside, white inside, with "walls" perforated by differently sized openings that function as windows. These miniature spaces serve as image carriers of Casanova + Hernandez's recently completed *Black and White Twins* and *Ginkgo Project* housing complexes, and can be equally understood as a work manifesto.

The architects' focus is less on the function of habitation and more on the question of which simple measures can be used to modulate the perception of simple forms. Whereas the solution is a geometric, subtly structured facade for the *Black and White Twins*, the seemingly playful ornament of an impressive glass facade defines the *Ginkgo Project*. The concept of changing perceptions resulting from varying spatial distances is of special importance. Only upon close inspection does the *Black and White Twins* facade reveal itself as an artful texture of overlapping linear structures. Developed from both the positioning of windows—mirroring interior function—and parameters of facade materials, this texture can be read as an abstract reference to the division of the surrounding building lots. On a huge open space, lacking significant landmarks, a shape had to be created, resulting in a striking urban structure. The *Ginkgo Project*'s stock of buildings, on the other hand, is defined on one side by an existing residential estate, on the other by a beautiful park with old trees. In spite of the almost diametric formulation of the facade details, which the architects call the "skin," here as a rationalist theoretical exercise, there as ornamental playfulness, they address the same idea: Both projects share the strategy of making perception and their order (from distance to proximity) a subject of focus.

The exhibition follows the same principle: Whereas the observer can only perceive a newly structured exhibition space from the distance, upon approaching s/he becomes aware of the differences in structure and their duality. Sensually ornamental on one side; rationally ordered on the other. Within both miniature structures, elements can be discovered that refer to details of the site and its usage. In the Ginkgo installation the elements are artificial grass covering the floor, a simple plastic chair and a potted plant—objects that are found on balconies around the world and with which people use to make their homes "nicer." In the Black and White installation on the other hand, photos and models are integrated. The miniature spaces thus breathe in the varying characteristics of both projects they represent through to the detail: the sensual in one, the rational in the other. The structured layers elucidate the credo of

architecture as "boxes" that share the same function, but covered by various layers can be interpreted in different ways. The "skin" as an architectural tool does not try to hide the true form behind it, but remains recognizable as a consciously designed membrane separating inside and outside. As central concepts of Casanova + Hernandez's architecture, scale and perception are transformed into the exhibition space through these artifacts, both concrete and abstract. This book serves to provide greater insight to this central theme of architecture.

Architecture at the Interface of Perception and Society

Claus Käpplinger

Helena Casanova and Jesus Hernandez, both from Madrid, combine the two most dynamic building cultures of the new millennium, from Spain and the Netherlands, and astonishingly enough founded their office in Rotterdam in 2001. Both architects studied at the Escuela Técnica Superior de Arquitectura de Madrid (ETSAM), where Rafael Moneo and Juan Navarro Baldeweg taught, among others. In the late nineties, Casanova and Hernandez resolutely made the move to the Netherlands to gain their first professional experience.
Knowing exactly what they were looking for, they first chose to work for the landscape architecture firm West 8. Casanova then moved on to Neutelings-Riedijk and Hernandez to Claus en Kaan, in order to understand other conceptual strategies better and in greater detail. They were particularly interested in the urban dimensions of architecture expanded by architectural landscape's relationship with the 21st century city, new urban interactions and perceptions, which were less prominent in Spanish architectural discourse. And it was mainly Dutch architects who focused on projects addressing hybridity, heterotopias and the development of new urban morphologies—projects that led many young architects from other countries to the Netherlands.
However, unlike most of the other visiting architects, Helena Casanova and Jesus Hernandez remained in the Netherlands. A successful entry to a European competition in Groningen (an urban planning project!) in 2001 offered them the opportunity to start their own Rotterdam office. That more than a decade would pass until the first section of the Groningen project would be constructed was unforeseeable. The two Spanish architects were astonishingly successful at understanding how to steer their office through the vicissitudes of Dutch architectural culture of the last decade. The end of the golden era of the polder model, several economic crises, and the assassination of right-wing populist Pim van Fortuyn forced more pragmatism and realism into the field. The Casanova/Hernandez generation operates today in other, more pragmatic, though equally conceptual strategies, now dealing more with the social reality of their present, where shrinking budgets, social differences and questions of identity require new models for solutions.
"Architecture must serve society," is a Casanova + Hernandez Architecten statement that shapes their projects and conceptual paths. Perception and human perception, but also transmutation and communication are central to their work. Their goal is not the autonomous object, but rather the set of related objects and the subjects with the objects; for which they always take unusual paths, such as the development of architectural landscape interventions.
The "Green Room," half open and half closed, architectural, botanical and urban seating at the same time, has been migrating around Rotterdam since 2009. It decidedly challenges passersby to interact, change the way they see the familiar and appropriate space inside and outside of the room (formed by only two walls) into a very individual experience. Their "green room" allows playful exploration of boundaries between private and public spheres. French anthropologist Marc Augé defined "non-places" as interchangeable places where the individual feels ambivalent and has no sense of belonging. Through targeted interventions, Casanova + Hernandez transform these non-places into places that can be connected again with interactions and memories.

Breaking viewing habits through very sensual information medias or filters of varying legibility and meaning is also detectable in Casanova+Hernandez's real architectural work. They have developed a unique methodology for the development and communication of their projects. In response to policy regarding usage (economic and otherwise), a client's often narrow specifications, or desired materials and appearance of a project, the architects do not just respond with plans and building code numbers. Contrary to dominant, present-day reasoning they try to approach the appropriate solution for site and program through sensually condensed ideas.

The ideas flow first into small objects that can be easily held in one's hand, to stimulate dialogue and interpretations. Space and structure found in these objects become condensed integral analogies, physically tangible but still variable. A translucent block, a solid stone with incised infill or, what is at first glimpse, just an unraveled strip of cardboard enables the particular shape of a project idea to emerge amazingly clearly. The objects are invitations to dialogues about the desired relations between interior and exterior. They represent architecture whose space is not conceived of serially added parts, but from the perception of an entirety. The reason why Casanova + Hernandez use subtraction is to achieve close interlinkage of site and program from the design of different spaces and interfaces between privacy and the public sphere later in the process.

In the Blaricummermeent settlement, a polder area without distinguishable identity or history, the architects were faced with the task of creating two multi-family housing blocks in a new neighborhood of single-family homes. Surrounded by water on two sides, the area offered only the attractiveness of the nearby water landscape as a dominant quality in the project. Breaking up the large building mass using prominent openings created various perspectives into the landscape. A perforated casing should be perceived more so than the building mass. Casanova + Hernandez thus generated the idea of an endless belt that—with its apertures of differing scale and depth—is read visually as a community of individual units.

The striking black cladding and white cuts into the volumes of the *Black and White Twins* stand by no means in opposition to each other. Together they fulfill the houses' function complementarily with the outside space. The shell is perceived as a filter; the volume more as space and less as a mass. The perforations—ultimately developed from a modular system of window openings—interlock interior and exterior in a refreshing way. They invite reading the internal spatial structure on the facade—through which the light enters very differently—and the size of the opening in relation to the space behind it. Beyond that, the flexibility of the concept made construction of 14 condos in one of the Twins and 15 apartments in the other, possible in the same volume. Positioned on two edges of the Blaricummermeent development, they are landmarks forgoing overwhelming dominance. They are two independently recognizable buildings and a calm visual presence.

The *Ginkgo Project*, on the other hand, is implanted in a residential area of postwar Beekbergen near Apeldoorn. In this case as well, the architects were confronted with the task of urban densification, this time between a park and single-family homes. Here too, the difference in scale between the existing and desired spatial program—to create affordable apartments (including housing for people over 65)—was a factor. The architects divided the program into two very differently dimensioned building masses, a four-story multiple-family house and a group of row houses. The result is a small ensemble whose skins were applied once again as an interface to visually shrink the building mass and strengthen identity. An integrated, artificial skin of glass, printed with a botanical pattern, enables the building mass to melt in with the nearby park, whereas its clinker-clad street front and similarly dimensioned window openings reference the characteristics of its neighboring buildings.
The glass "ginkgo fields" and their fragile branches envelop the building mass like a filter and veil of varying transparency, immateriality and profile depending on the height of the sun and weather conditions. The significant depth and mass—of the four-story building in particular—disappears behind this veil. Four rings radiate out from the core. The first spatial zone houses technical services for the entire building. The second ring accommodates services for baths and kitchens. The third is composed of variable loft-like living space to flow out to the balconies, as an outdoor extension of living space forming the last ring. A specific organization of floor plans consistent throughout Casanova + Hernandez's work enables extraordinarily compact, flexible and efficient floor plans.
The architects designed floor plans accommodating the construction of affordable living space in Beekbergen for 1,200 euro per square meter, that betray a profound examination of contemporary living and the desire for greater individuality in new communities. For years, they have dedicated themselves with a rare intensity to questions surrounding living and public space that reaches far beyond the architectonic object, and includes public furniture, city planning, landscape and society as a whole.

Casanova + Hernandez advocate a reflective modernity through their buildings, numerous texts and teaching engagements such as at the renowned Berlage Institute in Rotterdam. They advocate a modernity that dares to do experiments and question itself, and pragmatically and creatively promotes social change. The title of their book Public Space Acupuncture, in which they work together with sociologist Arnold Reijndorp, should also be understood as thoroughly programmatic. As a modification of the French term "intellectuel engagé" one can describe them as socially and culturally engaged architects who are building a ceramics museum and garden in China and who won a competition for a high-rise in the center of Rotterdam, all while initiating discourse about the city and its society.

The Black and White Twins

Housing in Blaricum

Site plan 1:2000

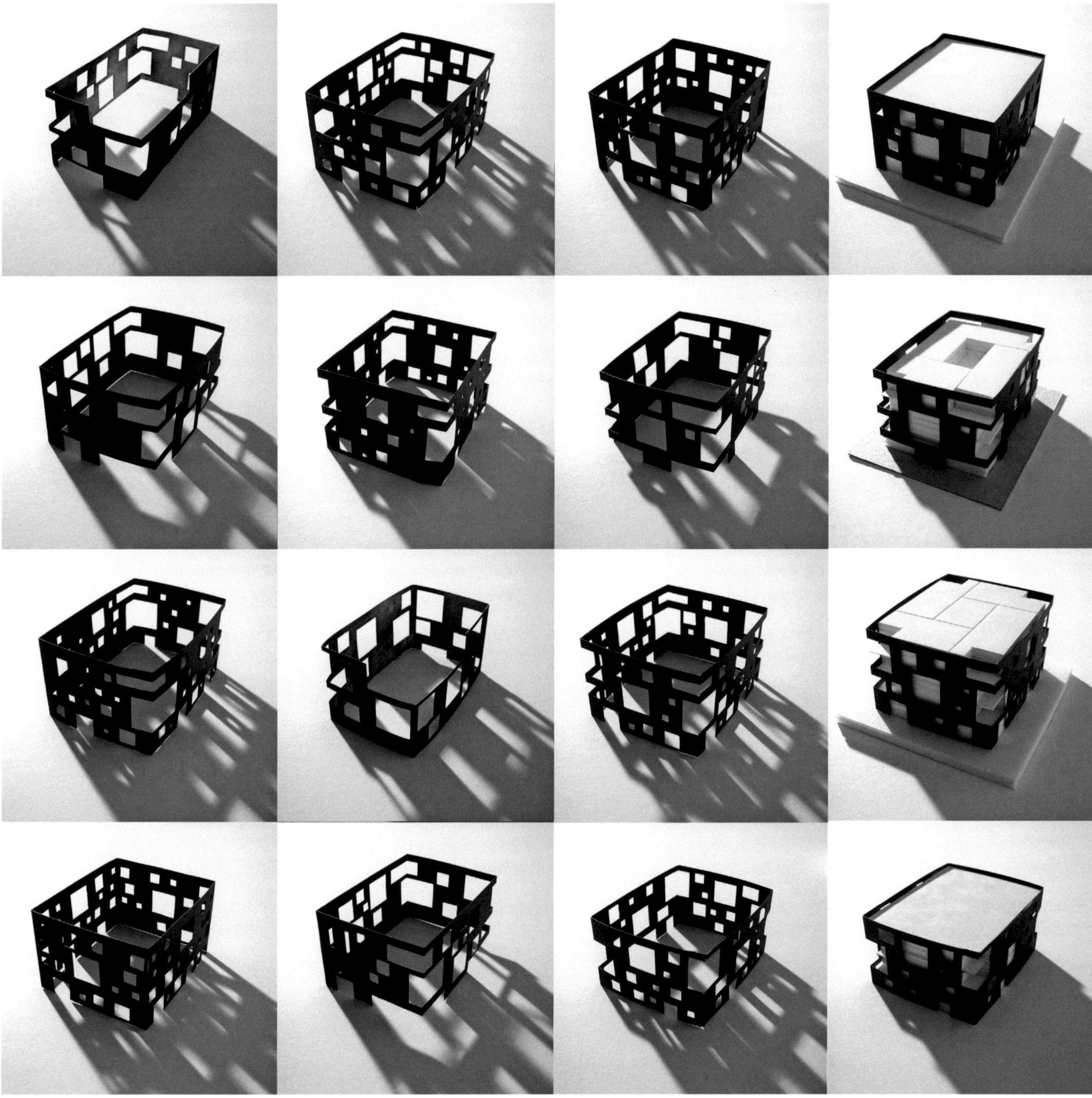

Study models

The mass

The skin

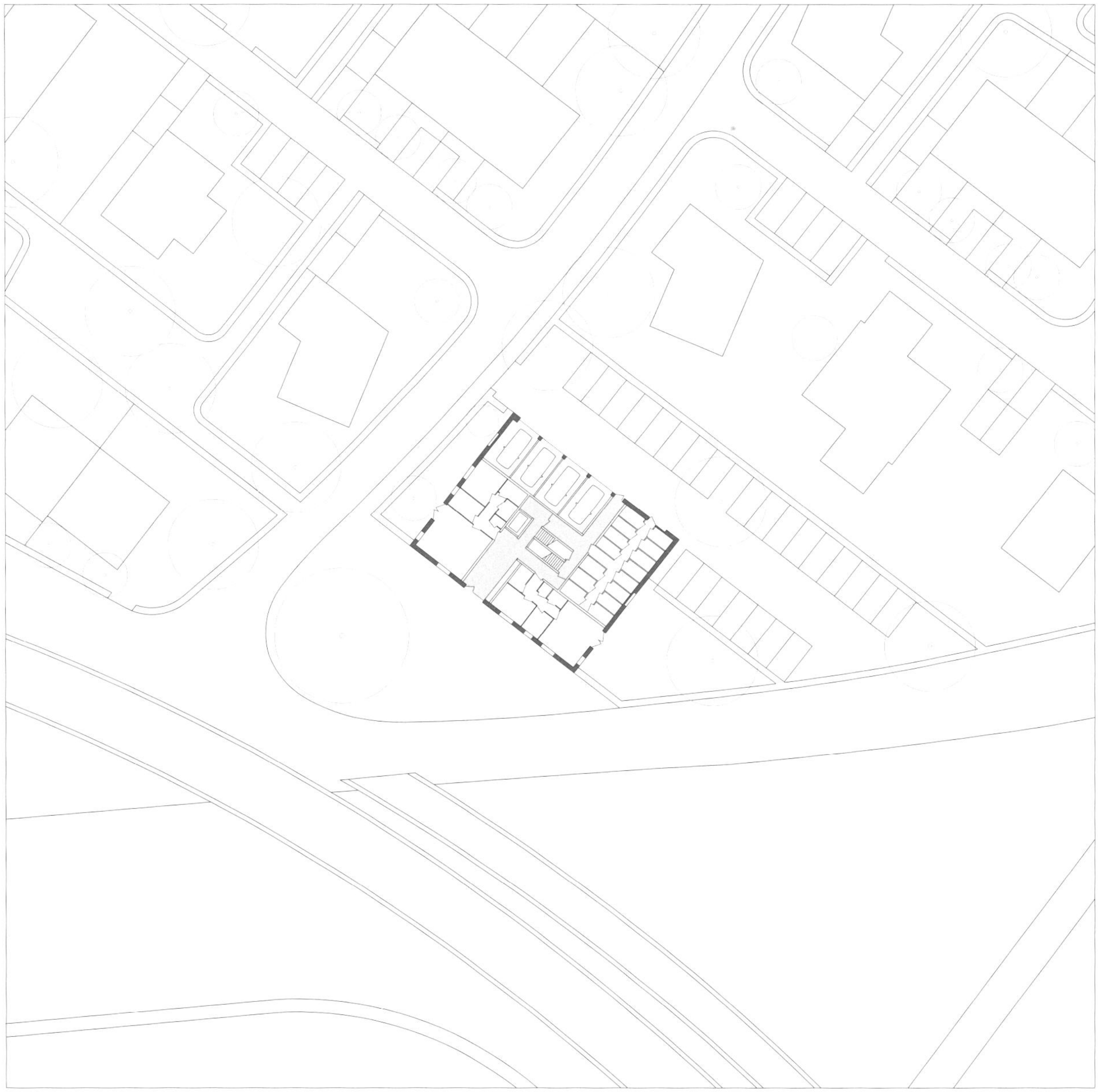

Site plan Block A   1:750

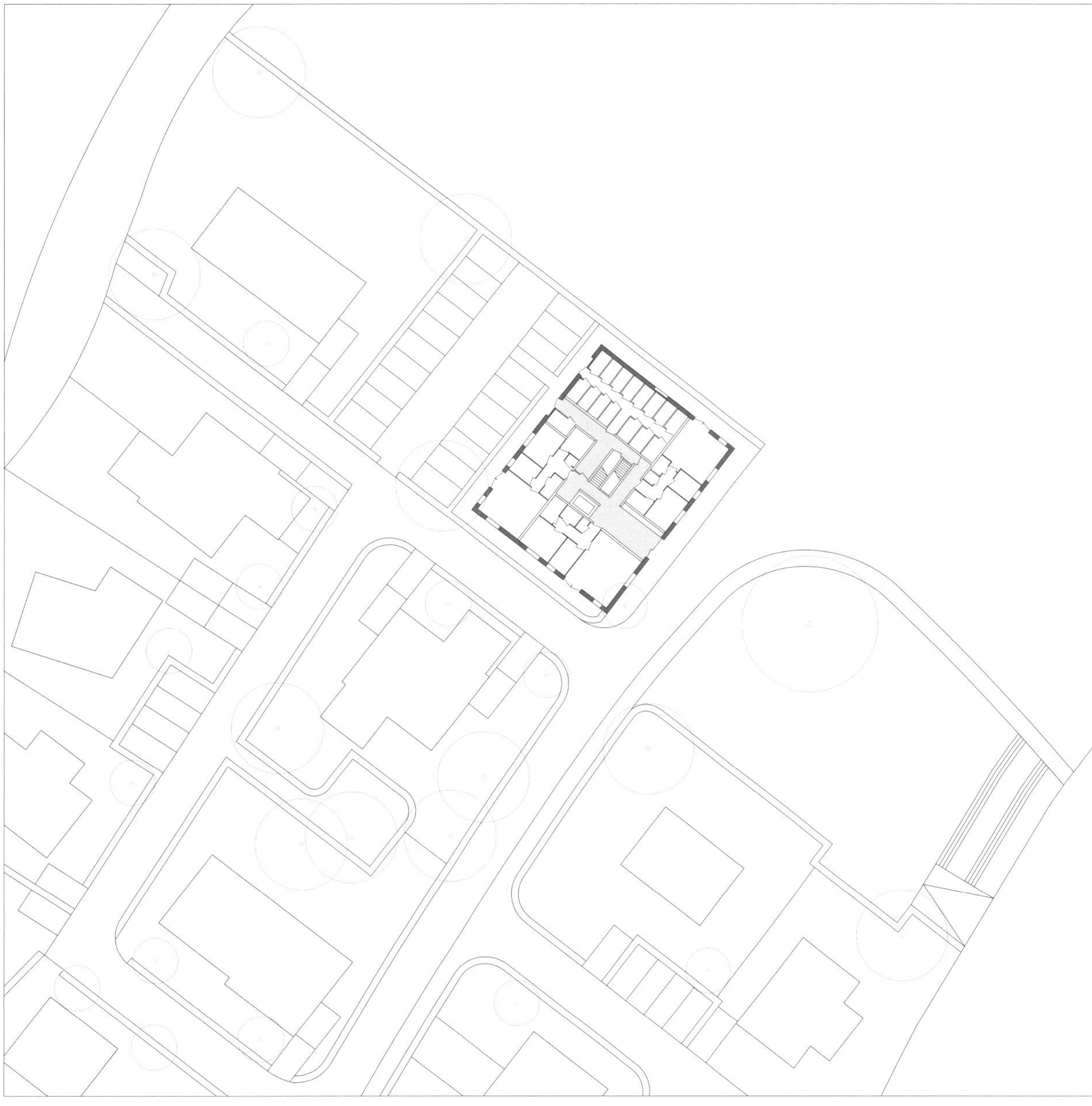

Site plan Block B   1:750

First floor +3.00 m 1:200

Third floor +9.00 m   1:200

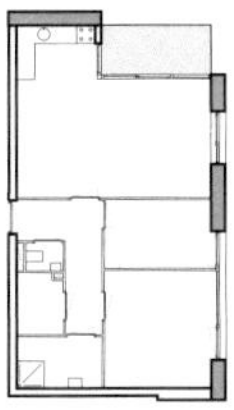

4a

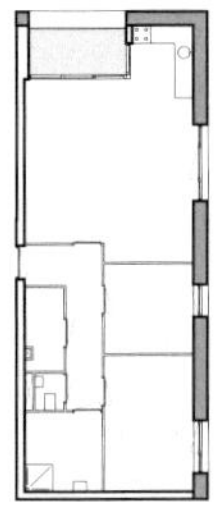

4b

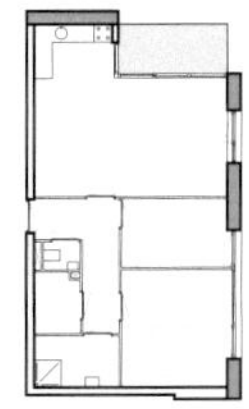

4c

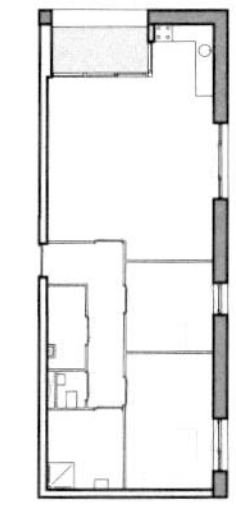

4d

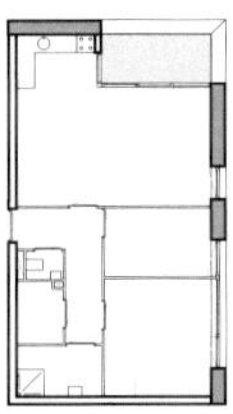

3a

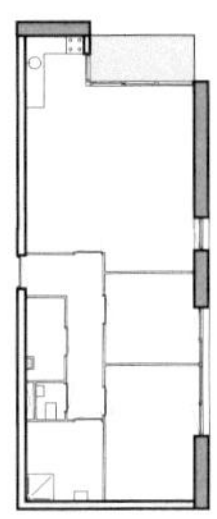

3b

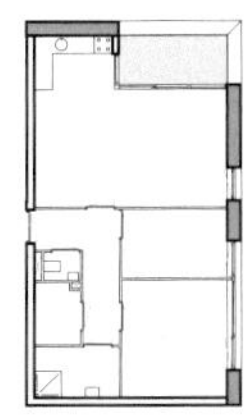

3c

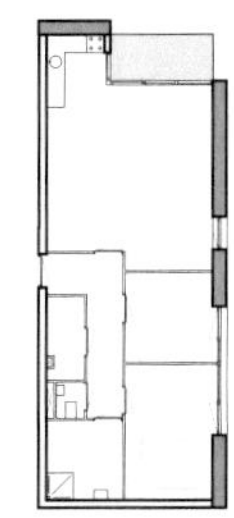

3d

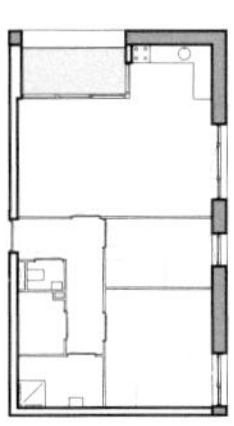

2a

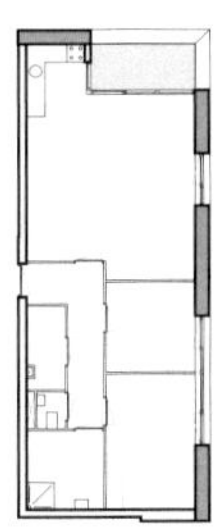

2b

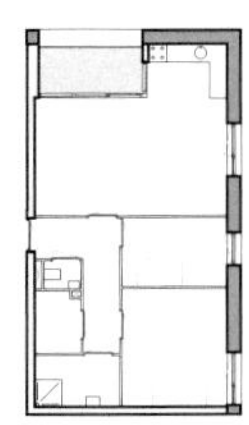

2c

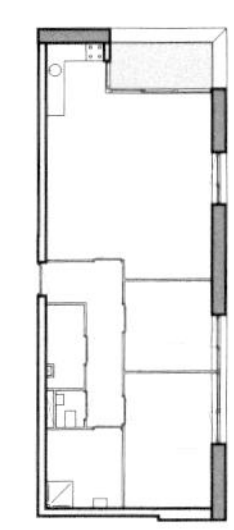

2d

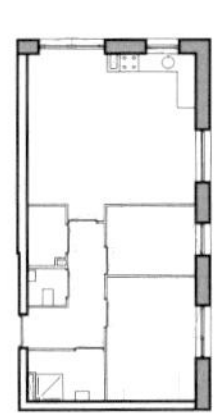

1b

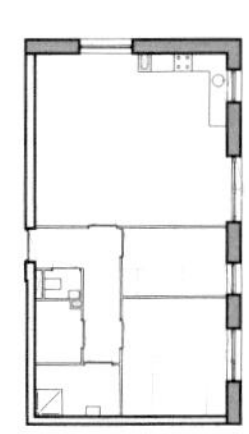

1c

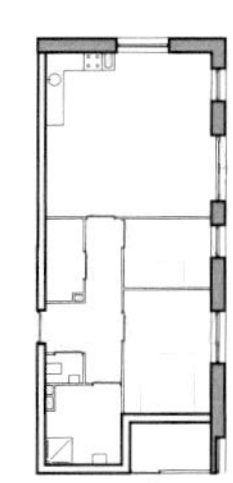

1d

Housing types 1:500

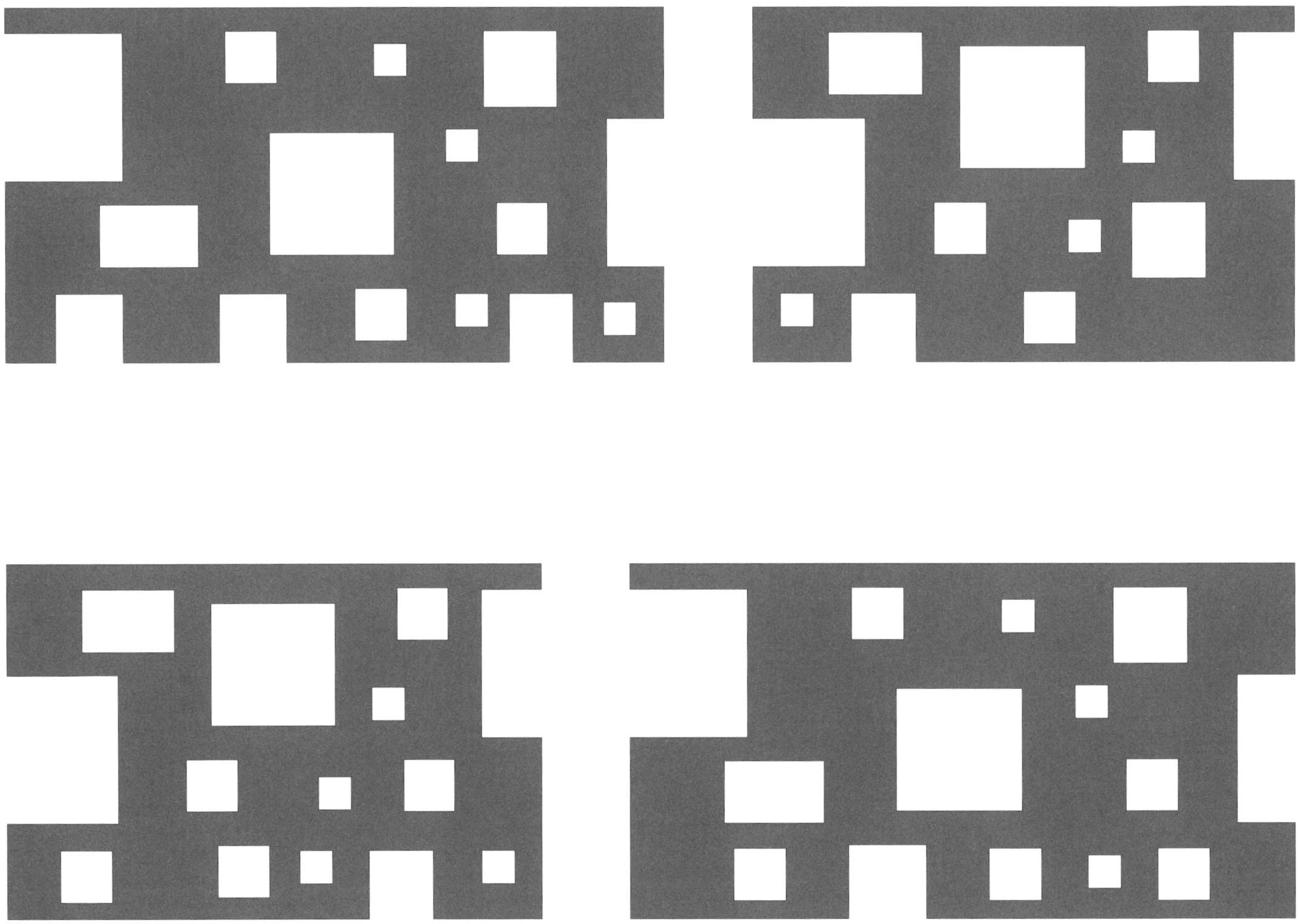

Perforated skin   1:250

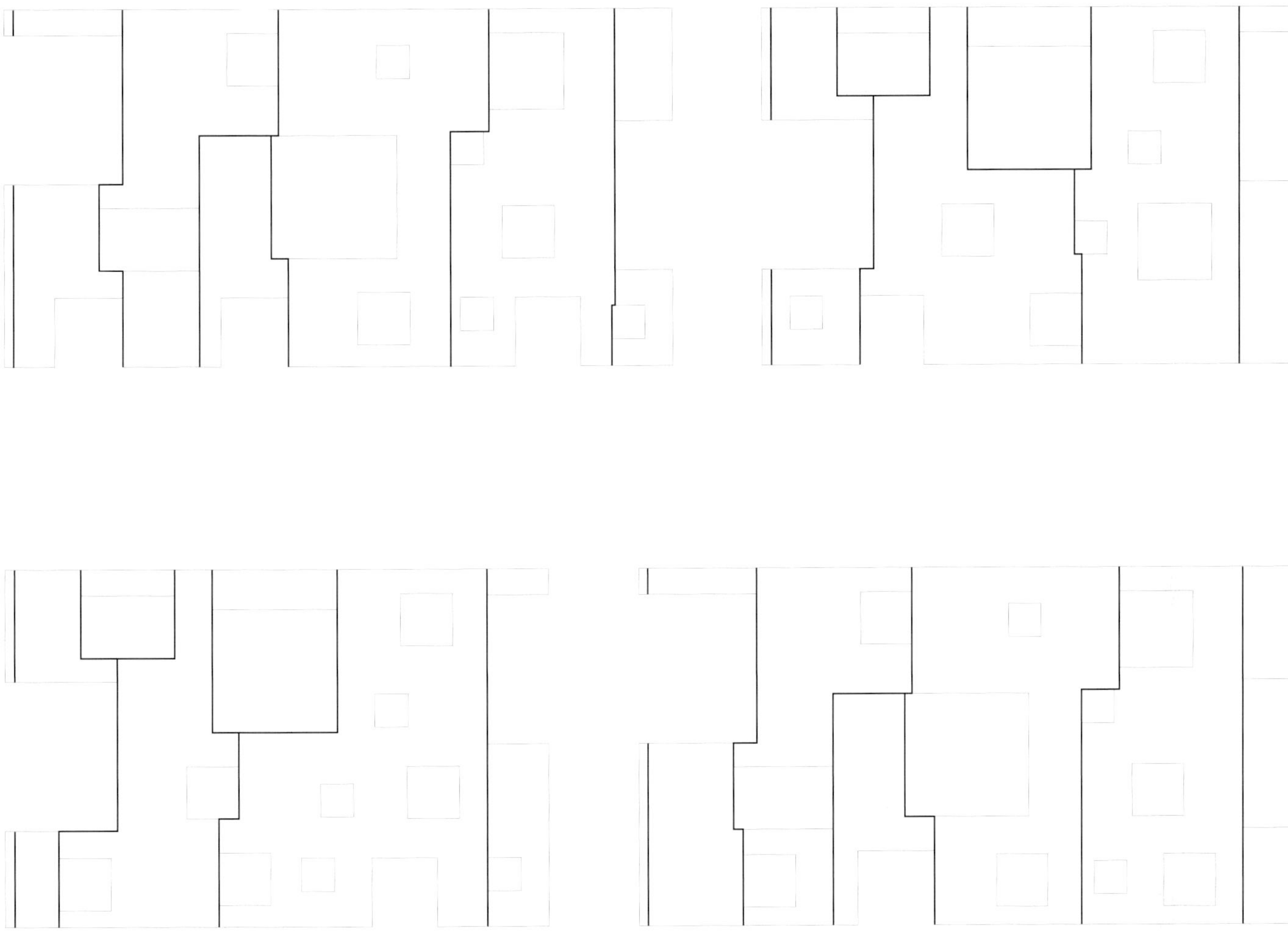

Expansion joints 1:250

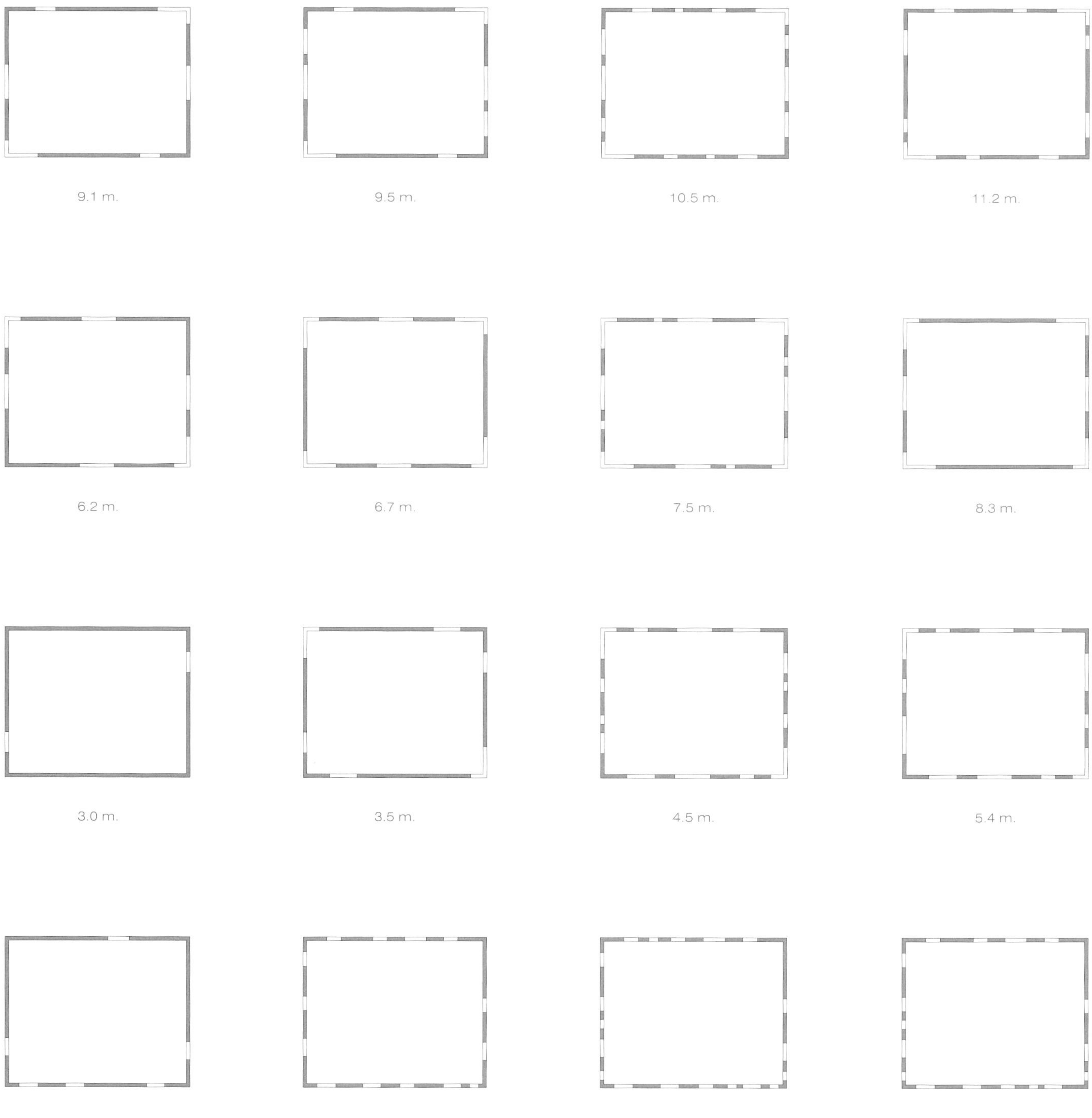

The Skin. 16 horizontal sections   1:750

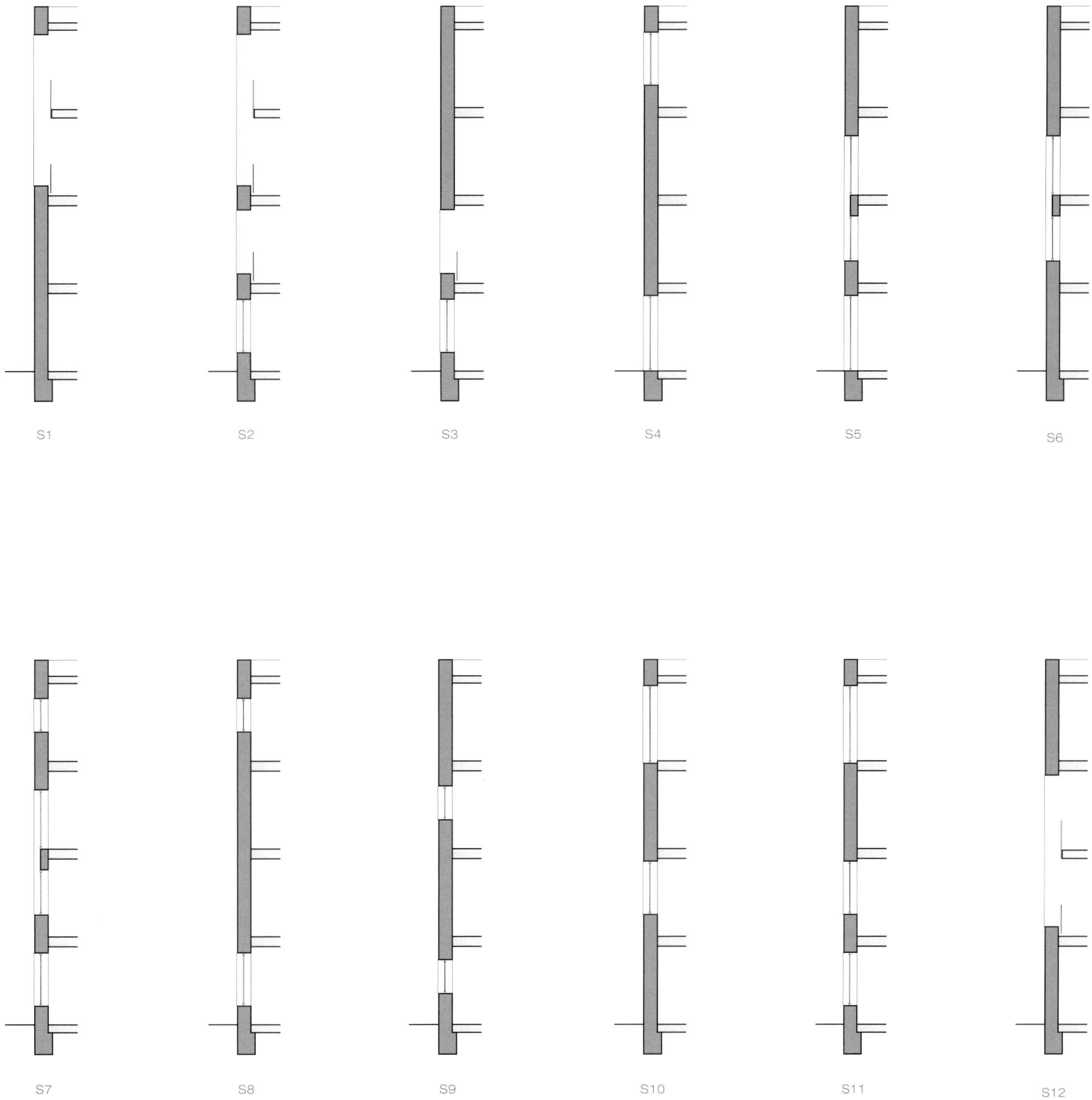

The Skin. 12 vertical sections 1:200

Elevations   1:250

Window frame types 1:100

Relationship between facade and interior 1:250

Relationship between windows and interior 1:150

The Ginkgo Project

Housing in Beekbergen

Site plan 1:5000

Conceptual model

Site plan 1:750

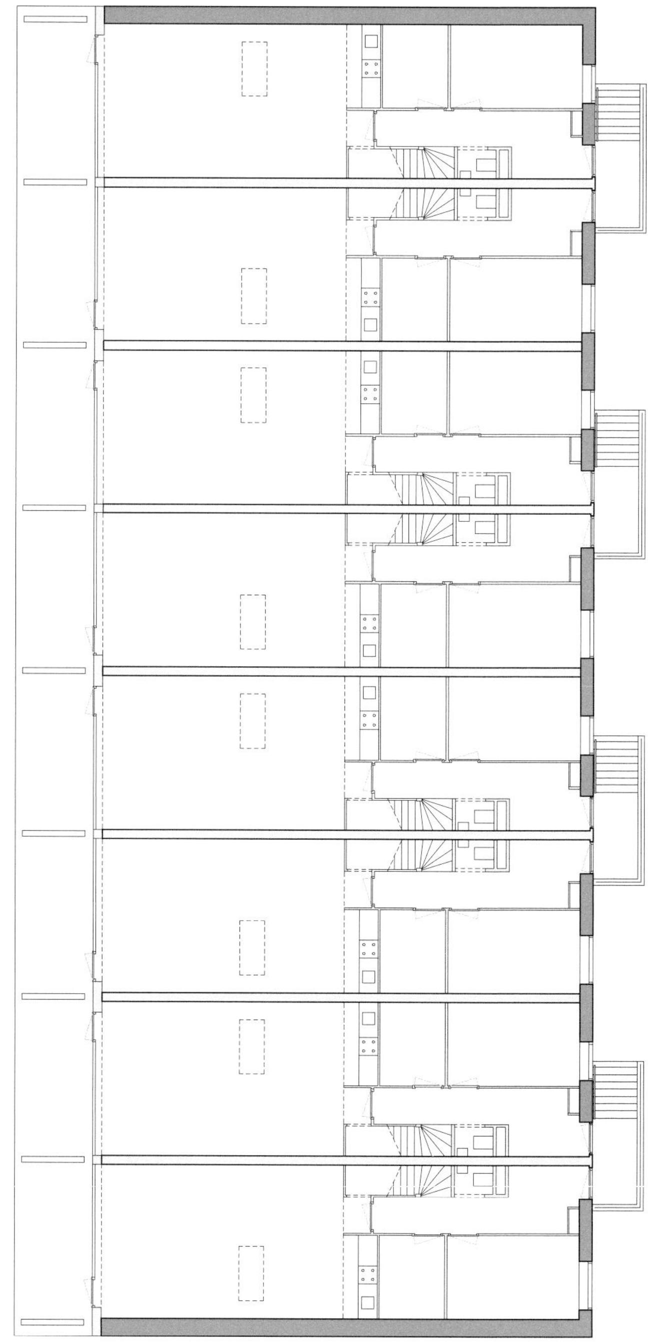

Park dwellings / ground floor +1.50m   1:250

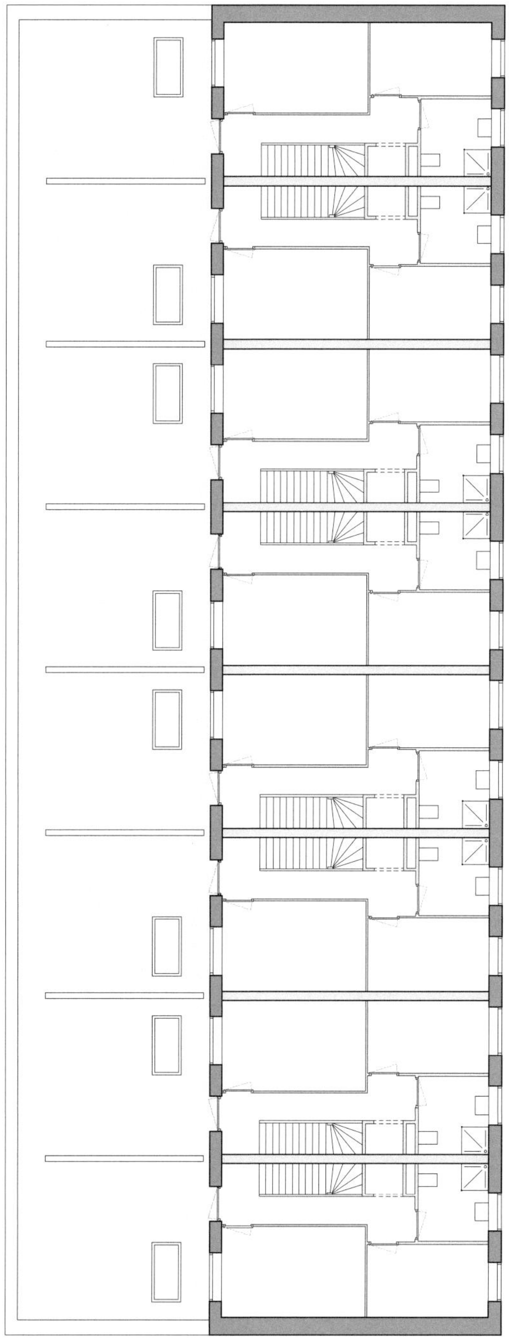

Park dwellings / first floor +4.50 m   1:250

Park dwellings / park facade   1:250

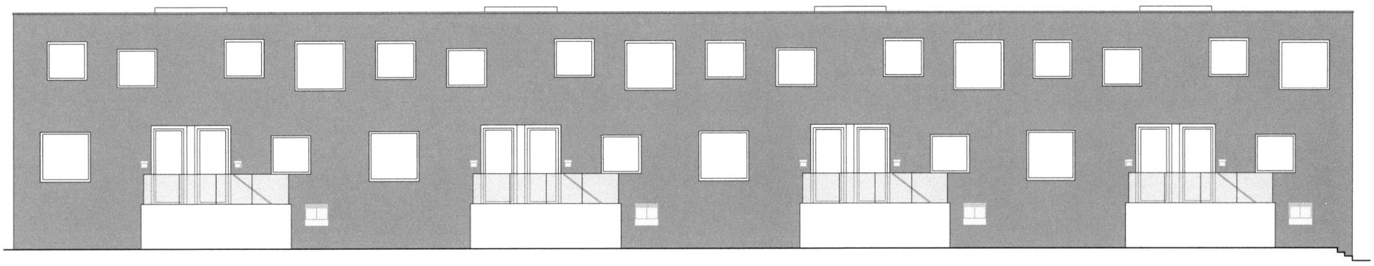

Park dwellings / street facade 1:250

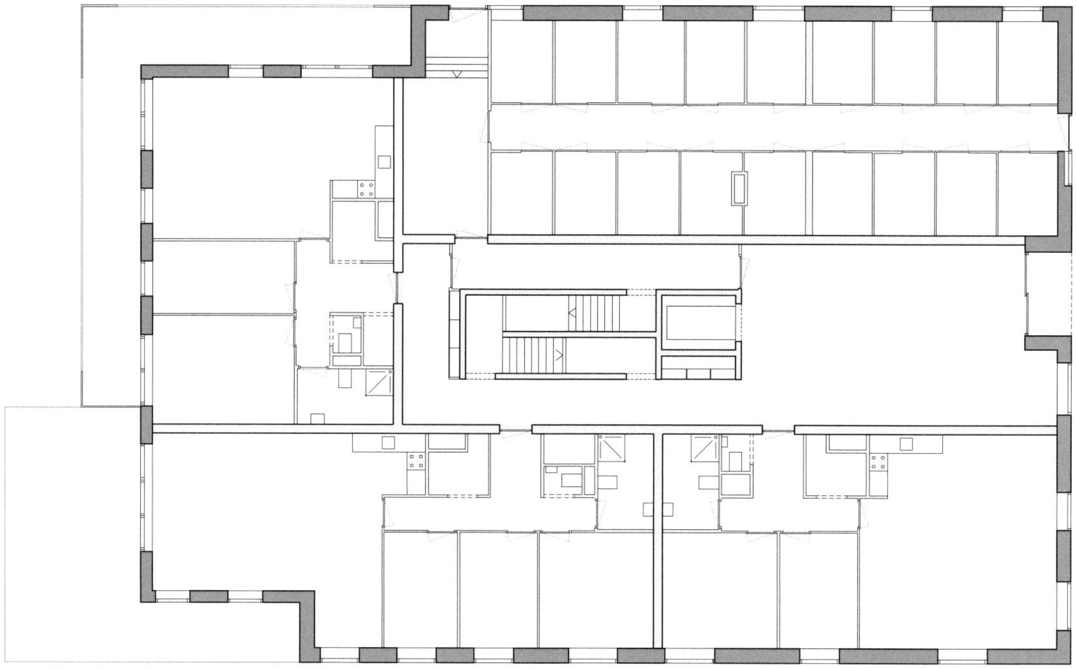

Housing block / ground floor +1.50 m   1:250

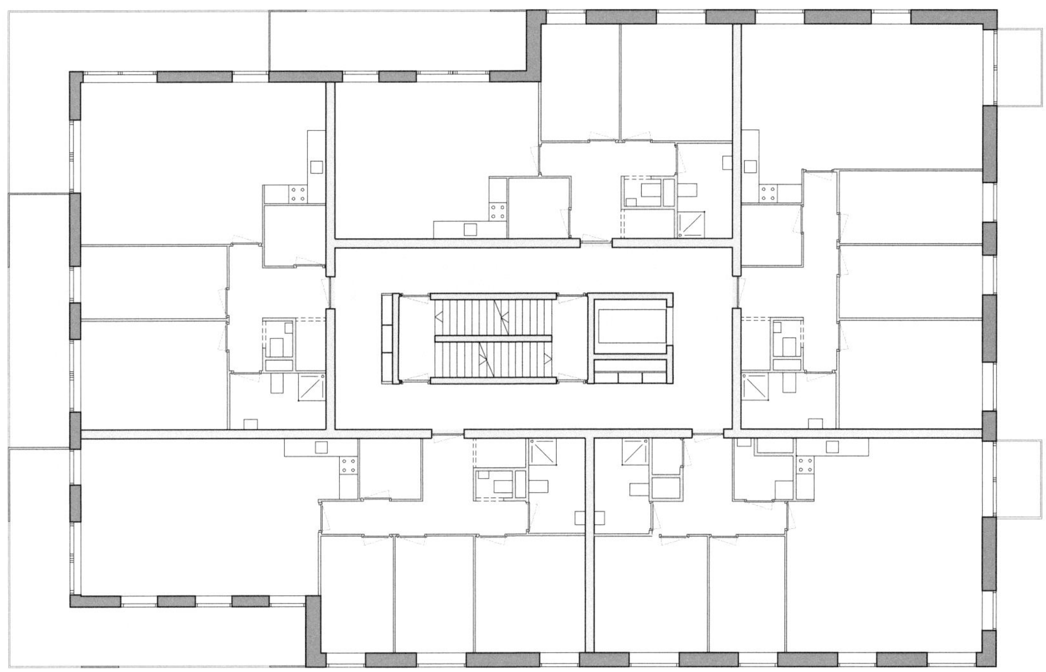

Housing block / first floor +4.50 m   1:250

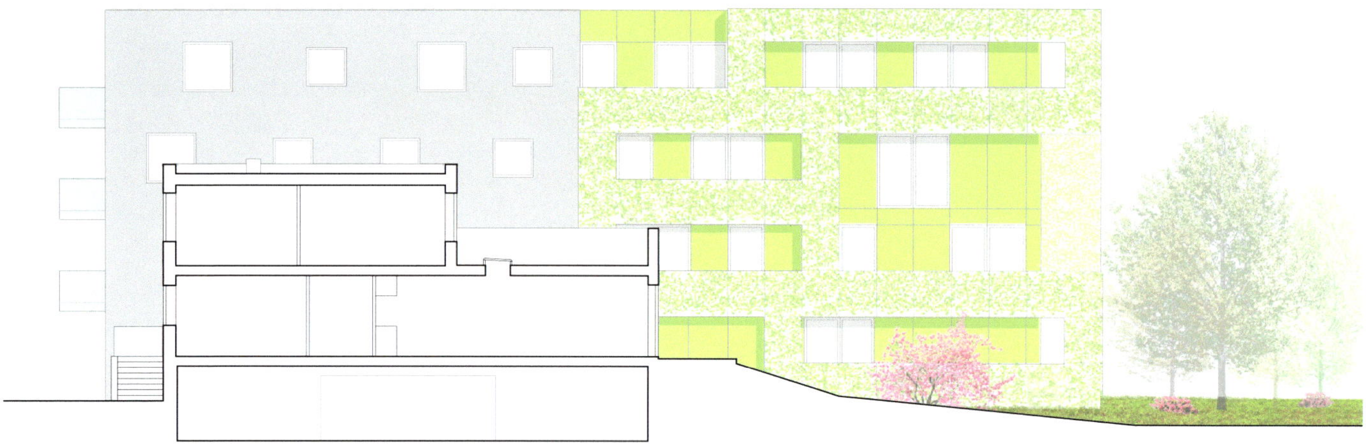

Section elevation 1:250

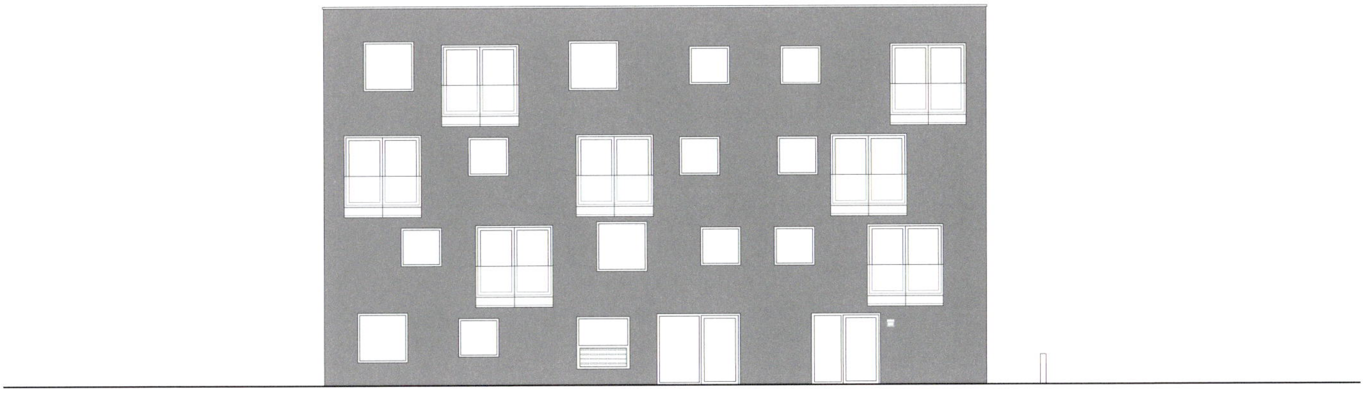

Housing block / park and street facades 1:250

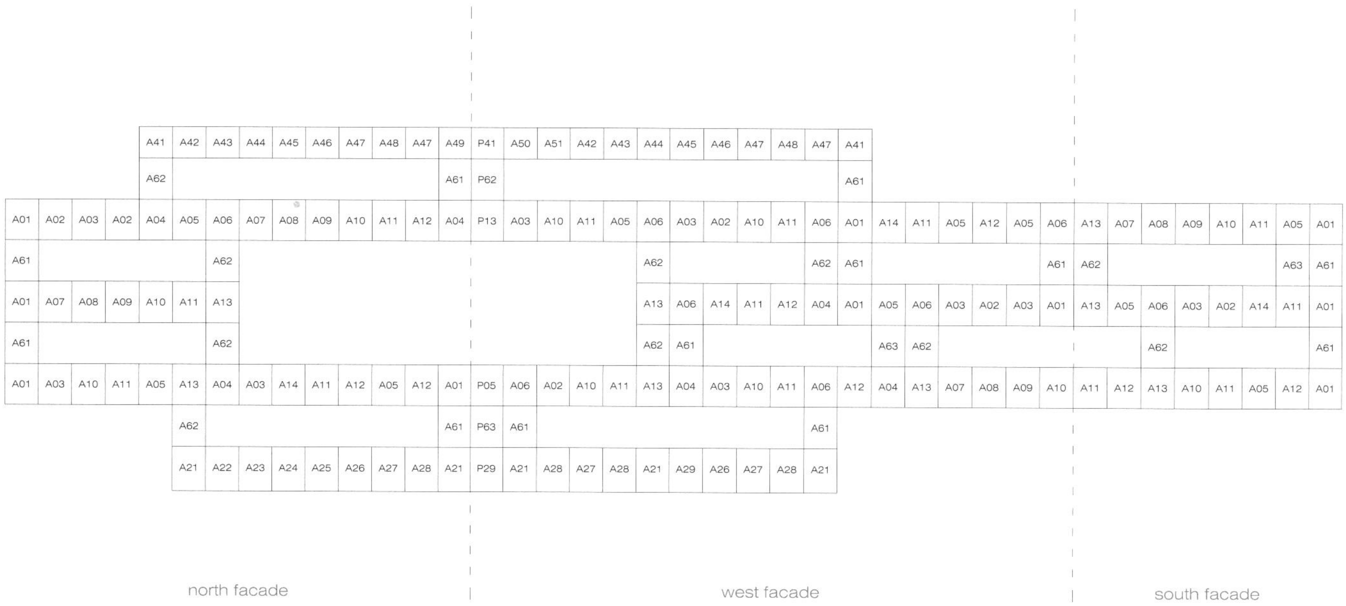

Housing block / unfolded printed glass skin – print codes 1:275

Housing block / unfolded printed glass skin 1:275

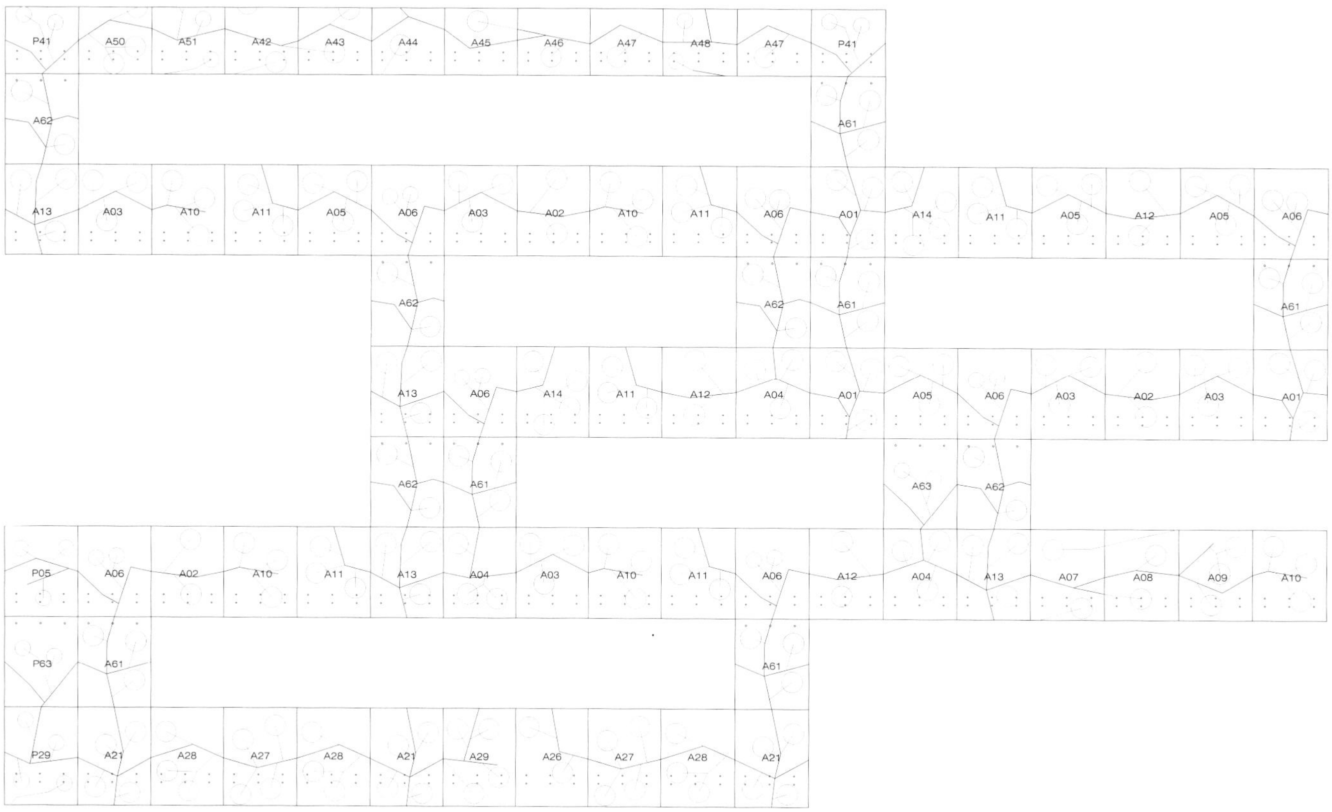

Housing block / west facade printed glass skin – print codes 1:125

Housing block / west facade printed glass skin   1:125

B01

B02

B03

B04

B05

B06

B07

B08

B09

B10

B11

B12

B13

B16

B17

Park dwellings / catalogue of printed glass panels 1:40

A01

A02

A03

A04

A05

A06

A07

A08

A09

A10

A11

A12

A21

A22

A23

A29

Housing block / catalogue of printed glass panels 1:40

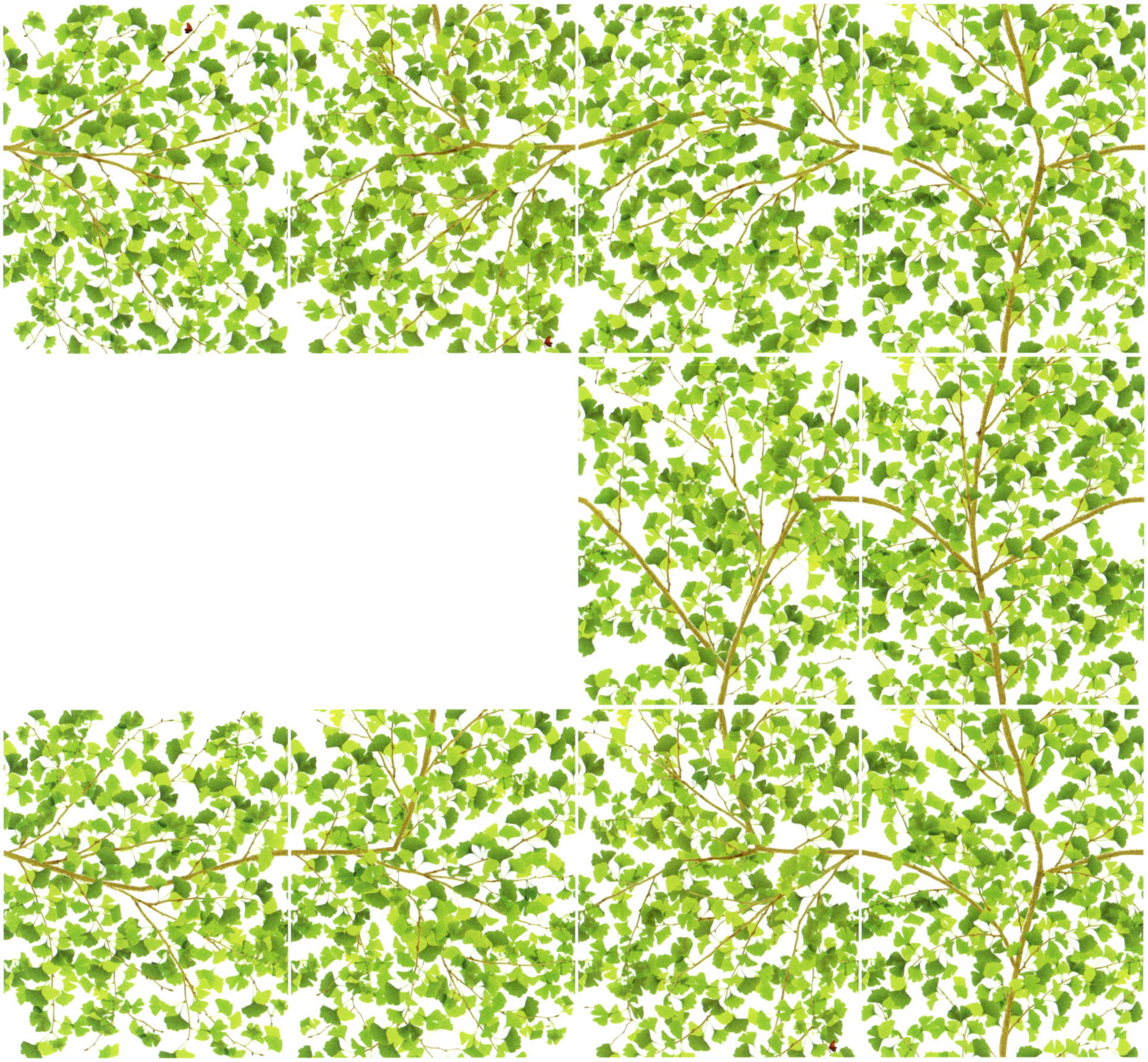

Syntax scheme of printed glass skin / fragment   1:30

Fixation of printed glass skin 1:15

Detail 1 of printed glass skin 1:11

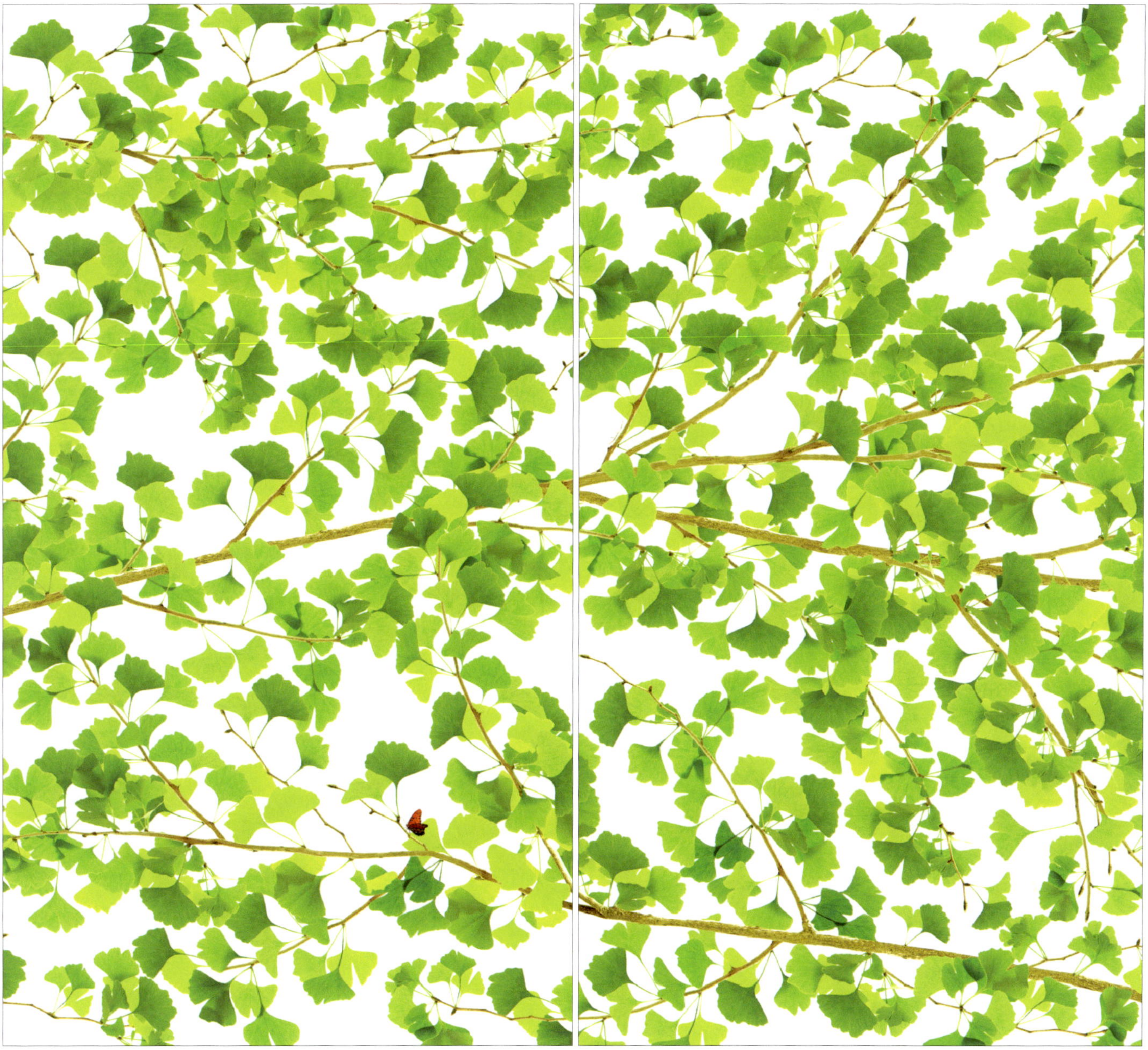

Detail 2 of printed glass skin 1:11

Ginkgo print motif 1:1

Scale & Perception: Rethinking Phenomenological Architecture in the Global Age

Helena Casanova / Jesus Hernandez

Architects often focus on designing objects instead of designing the perception of the objects. The term perception refers to the act of identifying and interpreting sensory information in order to understand the environment. Although perception is frequently understood as visual perception only, it does in fact involve the use of all our senses. Stephen Holl stated in Questions of Perception. Phenomenology of Architecture that "although cinema has a strong emotional potential, only architecture is capable of awakening simultaneously all the senses, all the complexity of perception". This complexity is caused not only by the superposition of multiple stimuli captured by the different sensory organs, but also by the change of those stimuli over the time. The visual perception of an object does not remain constant; on the contrary, it varies depending on the point of view and the changing atmospheric conditions during the day and with the seasons of the year.

The perception of an object is a subjective act. In that sense subjectivism is related to the Berkeley's empiricist idealism that held that things only exist to the extent that they are perceived. The subjective approach to design in architecture understands the building not as a single object, but as hundreds of overlapping objects designed to produce in the subject hundreds of perceptions. The subjective understanding of architecture rethinks every aspect of the design as an independent entity that has a meaning by itself and contributes, in combination with others aspects, to provide the holistic dimension of architecture.

Phenomenological architecture is deeply concerned with the perception of buildings and the relation between the building and its place. But this subjective approach clashes strongly with generic solutions that in our global age are highly successful in market economies. In contemporary society the global and the local have entered into conflict with each other, and this conflict is also present in the field of architecture.

Over the last century, Fordism promoted experimentation with generic structural solutions like the concrete skeleton and architectonic prototypes like the Unité d'Habitation as ways of solving global problems such as affordable and hygienic housing. These solutions were then cloned around the world and very often conflicted with their locality. Paradoxically, in our current Post-Fordist society in which industry has the capacity to personalize production, global architecture produces similar cities all around the world, this time not created by the repetition of almost identical prismatic buildings, but by the cacophonic accumulation of an infinite variety of shaped buildings structured in what Rem Koolhaas named the generic city.

But why does current standardized contemporary architecture apparently follow practically the same principles around the world and relegate to a secondary plane basic aspects such as perception or the relation with the place? Should phenomenological architecture be restricted just to the field of exemplary small-scale housing and some public buildings? Or could it be rethought and implemented in collective housing projects that represent the larger construction demand in our increasingly urbanized world? Could explorations of subjectivism in architecture provide new tools, not only strictly phenomenological but also functional, to address the new socio-economic problems in very sensitive contexts?

The collective housing projects Ginkgo and Black & White, developed in the Dutch localities of Beekbergen and Blaricum, explore not only the architectural potential of scale and perception, but also, and equally importantly, the potential of rethinking the phenomenological approach towards architecture to create a successful response to global social demands with special attention for the specific problems of both places.

Beekbergen, like many other Dutch villages and towns in the Netherlands, consists mainly of large single-family houses, two or three floors in height. The lack of affordable housing forces young people who cannot afford to buy one of these big houses in the village to look for smaller apartments in cities nearby. At the same time, seniors have to contend with problems of mobility and, as a result, cannot make full use of their large three-level home. However, they cannot find smaller apartments with lifts in their local village. Because the cost of the land is very high, the only feasible solution to the problem is to create modern and dense multilevel housing complexes with affordable medium- and small-sized apartments. But the village residents often react against this kind of project, which are not sensitive to the scale and identity of the place. In this paradoxical context, generic modern residential blocks with no relation to the place or typical local low-density architecture cannot respond to all the demands. The solution has to provide creative ideas on scale and perception to be successful, creating architecture that is visually integrated into the place and, at the same time, capable of creating a dialogue with it.

Blaricummermeent is, by contrast, a new housing development of 900 dwellings situated in the north of the village of Blaricum. It consists for the most part of single-family homes and some row houses with gardens. In the first phase of the urban development, the Black & White buildings are the only two dense housing blocks in the area that try to combine many affordable apartments and whose volumes should not disturb the low-rise identity of the new area. In both cases, rethinking the role of phenomenological architecture could provide new sensitive and functional tools to experiment with scale and perception and address current social problems in relation to the context. Some of these tools can be summarized in the next five points.

1 Sense of scale: rescaling perception

Over the course of history, architects have developed sophisticated mechanisms to control and even manipulate the visual perception of the buildings. The Greek temple is a delicate piece of art designed to produce in the observer a perfect perception of the object. To compensate for the distorted visual perception that man has of reality, the architects designed different parts of the building with delicate curves.

The slight parabolic upward curvature of the stylobate, the entasis of the columns that compensate for the illusion of concavity, the slight tilting of the columns inwards, the tapering of the naos walls and the curvature of the architrave are all what experts like Gorham Stevens term 'optical refinements' that serve as a 'reverse optical illusion'.

If the Parthenon produces the illusion of perfection, the stage of the Teatro Olimpico of Vicenza designed by Vicenzo Scamozzi in 1585 creates the illusion of deepness. False perspective is used in this case to provide the illusion of the seven long streets envisioned by Andrea Palladio before his death, while the sets are actually just a few metres deep. The development of several treatises on perspective by theorists such as Leon Battista Alberti and Piero della Francesca during the Renaissance provided designers with new tools to experiment with and to model perception in architecture, which has continued evolving until the present day.

The design of the Parthenon and the Teatro Olimpico illustrates how the perception of a building is independent of its physical shape. According to Merlau-Ponty, 'the form of the objects is not their geometrical shape'. Two buildings with identical volumes and geometry could be perceived as larger or smaller, higher or lower, and longer or shorter ones depending on factors such as their specific composition, colour and materials. Over the history of architecture, many public or religious buildings have been designed to be perceived by citizens as edifices that appear larger than they were in reality. By contrast, architectural design can be also used to reduce the visual appearance of a building.

We understand the size of objects by comparing their dimensions with the dimensions of objects with which we are familiar. The sense of scale of an object is primarily acquired by comparing the object with the size of our body. The dimensions of the human body have often been the instrument to scale architecture. Many civilizations used the dimensions of parts of the human body such as fingers, palms, hands and feet to proportion architecture. The traditional Japanese house is modulated according to the dimensions of the tatami, which is created in relation to our body dimensions. The tatami therefore relates the dimensions of the house to the dimensions of the human body.

Objects existing in the physical context of buildings also provide a certain consciousness concerning the scale of architecture when it is not possible to compare it to human dimensions. The size of the nearby houses, urban elements or vegetation gives a sense of scale. Moreover, the dimensions of the common elements that form the building facade, such as windows and especially doors, give an indirect sense of scale because they are usually dimensioned according to the size of the human body. But while the tatami has standardized dimensions, building elements such as doors and windows can vary slightly in size and proportion and create an incorrect sense of the scale of the building.

During the design process of a building the conscious manipulation of the apparent scale of some facade components can lead to interesting changes in the perception of the scale of the whole building. For instance, there is a series of mechanisms experimented in the facade of the Black & White building that seek to reduce the apparent size of the building in order to visually integrate its volume with the scale of the low-rise residential urban context.

The 'extraction of mass' in this project from the ideal prismatic volume, especially when it is extracted from the four corners of the building, reduces its massive appearance. The white colour in the voids contrasts with the dark colour of the exterior facade to create what, according to the reification property of the gestalt theory, is called a subjective or illusory contour. As happens in many carved wooden sculptures created by Barbara Hepworth during the 1940s, colour helps to render visible the invisible and the void becomes an important constructive element of the work.

The black colour reinforces the appearance of the outer skin of the building and the white frames underline the presence of the voids perforated into it. On the one hand, the grouping of four windows of different apartments into a single opening minimizes the amount of windows perceived in the facade. On the other hand, the extra-large size of these openings visually reduces the scale of the building when its dimensions are compared to the unconventionally large size of the voids.

Experimentation with several aspects that relate scale and perception makes it possible to minimize the relative scale of a building and visually integrate a medium-size housing block into the small scale of the residential neighbourhood.

While the urban facade of the Ginkgo project is made of bricks and features windows of similar size to the ones of the nearby buildings to allow observers to identify the real scale of the building, its park facade is designed with mechanisms that manipulate the sense of scale in order to integrate the building into the natural context.

The image of the building when it is viewed from the park is articulated by a glazed printed skin that is independent of the real facade of the building. This glazed skin works not only as a balustrade to the long balconies that surround the building, but also as a visual interface. The sense of scale is reduced: first, by creating large double-height openings together with long openings in the skin, whose unusual sizes and proportions cannot be associated with those of standard windows; and second, by the abstract quality of the printed glazed skin, which in part reflects the surroundings, and by its minimalist construction, made without any components that could provide a reference dimension to understand its scale.

The Black & White project scales down the perception of the building by recoding the cognitive elements that allow us to obtain a sense of scale, but the Ginkgo project deactivates the standard mechanisms that normally provide a sense of scale, thus providing an open and subjective interpretation of the scale of the building in relation to the ambiguous scale of the surrounding nature. This open perception of the scale of architecture is also stimulated by the natural changes of the atmospheric conditions that provide infinite variations in the way natural light illuminates and creates reflections in the glazed skin of the building.

2 Scale and detail: gradual perception

The documentary film written and directed by Ray and Charles Eames in 1968 entitled Powers of Ten shows a continuous zoom-out from the image of a lakeside picnic in Chicago until the image of the universe. The image zooms out slowly at a rate of one power of ten per ten seconds. Each image of the film shows a scale and a level of detail related to a specific observation distance: one person one metre, a park 100 metres, the city 1000 metres and so on. In the words of the authors, the film deals 'with the relative size of things in the universe' and one could add that it also deals with the relative visual perception that we have of these things depending on the observation distance.

A piece of architecture is a small but complex universe formed by many interlinked parts that are designed at different scales depending on the perception distance. John Ruskin describes in his book Lectures on Architecture and Painting the adaptation of the ornamentation of Amiens Cathedral to its distance from the eye. The sculptural elements located near the observer's point of view present a high refinement of line and finish of edge, while the ornamentation of the niches positioned high in the building are more volumetric and create broad shadows that catch the eye instead.

Moreover, the classic Greek temple could be understood as an ensemble of many varied and differentiated elements. In contrast to Ruskin's observation about Amiens Cathedral, the level of detail of each element of the Greek temple does not always relate to the position of the element within the building. Instead, it depends on the distance from which the detail should be read. Two elements of the same building, such as the metopes and the sculptures of the pediment, are positioned very close to each other, but they have very different levels of detail to regulate the distance from which they should be fully appreciated. The pediment is designed to be visible from a longer distance and therefore it presents larger and more volumetric sculptures than the metopes. These parts have been articulated to act as sensorial tools that activate different parts of our perception depending on the observation distances, together creating a rich visual experience, not only from one viewpoint, but from many different angles and distances.

The fact that an object can be observed from many different distances and viewpoints generates many different perceptions of it. Merlau-Ponty stated in his book Phenomenology of Perception that 'for each object, as for each picture in an art gallery, there is an optimal distance from which it requires to be seen'.

It means that from that optimal distance we perceive the whole object and all its aspects. The 360-degree panoramic exhibition room of the Museum of History of Jinzhou in China displays a scene of the history of the city that mixes objects at scale one-to-one on the near plane with a panoramic hyperrealist painting on the cylindrical wall of the room on a second plane. The optimal distance between the observer and the wall was fixed at 13 metres because this is the distance from which, following some empirical studies, our vision starts to blur, mixing the perception of the real objects with the paintings on the wall. In this case, fixing the observation distance generates an illusion for the observer who perceives continuity between three-dimensional and two-dimensional representation.

Although the existing urban context around the buildings only allow us to observe them from a limited number of viewpoints and from certain distances, when we move approaching the building we experience a sequence of different perceptions in time. Following Merlau-Ponty, at certain distance we experience the optimal perception of the complete building, and moving from that position towards the building we perceive not only a fragmented view of the whole, but also details and information not perceived before. A gradual perception provides a coherent sequence of views by linking each observation distance to the adequate scale of design that allows the observer to perceive certain details. The gradual perception joins the far, medium and short distance views, linking space, time, material and detail.

The printed glazed skin of the Ginkgo project observed from a far distance visually integrates the building with the greenery of the park. In a closer view of its facade, the observer clearly perceives the realistic image of branches and leaves printed on the glass, which plays with the conscious and unconscious line that divides reality and illusion, nature and artifice, and art and architecture. In a close look at the facade, the observer discovers a universe of small details such as small insects camouflaged at different points along the branches that makes the building surprising, alive and unpredictable.

There are also different elements of the Black & White building that have been specially designed to consider different scales to be perceived from different distances: the scale of the context (1/1000), the near surroundings (1/500), the volume of the building (1/200), the facade (1/100), the elements of the facade (1/50), special elements (1/20), main details (1/5) and very special details (1/1). Observing the building from a long distance, the eye focuses on the sculptural character of the large corner voids of the building. As we approach the building our attention shifts to the geometrical composition of windows of different sizes and more subtle details such as the irregular geometrical drawings of the expansion joints that have been carefully designed in combination with the position of the windows. Finally, in a close view of the building we focus on its materials, colours and textures.

The gradual perception of the Black & White project is based on the physical adjustment of volume, colours, materials and textures, depending on the observation distance. By contrast, the gradual perception of the printed glass skin of the Ginkgo project rethinks the relation between the observation distance and the architecture from a virtual perspective, experimenting with scale and perception, not only in constructive terms, but also in artistic ones to add an extra layer to the architectural experience.

3 The whole and the parts: articulated perception

Aristotle illustrated the relation of the parts to the whole with the example of stones to a house. Nobody can understand a complete house by observing in isolation each stone of the house. The relation of part to whole and of part to part within a whole is studied in mereology. Although the ideas of Aristotle about the whole and the parts were further developed by medieval philosophers such as Thomas Aquinas and by Immanuel Kant, Franz Brentano was probably the first to formulate a theory of parthood relations in his book Descriptive Psychology in 1887. In his book, Brentano distinguished between 'dependent parts' and 'independent or separable parts', a concept that was further developed by Eduard Husserl in 1901 in his Third Logical Investigation in which he distinguished between concrete and abstract parts.
A building is also formed of different parts. Some of them are separable and others are dependent parts. Independently of the level of articulation of the architectural parts, the relation between dependent parts can produce what we can call the articulated perception of the architecture.

On the one hand, articulated perception affects all the senses, not only the view or the traditional five senses attributed to Aristotle (sight, hearing, touch, smell and taste), but also other senses such as balance or kinaesthetic sense. Articulated perception takes into account the relation among the parts and the complete multisensory experience. On the other hand, articulated perception links very different parts of the object which correspond to very different categories, such as physical constructive elements, colours or textures, establishing a complex set of relationships among parts within the same category, and also among the different categories and the whole.
The principle of totality, defined by the gestalt psychologist Kurt Koffka as 'the whole is other than the sum of the parts', states that conscious experience must be considered globally. Therefore, although each part is defined precisely and stands out clearly, articulation reveals how the parts relate to each other to create a holistic experience. Both buildings, Black & White and Ginkgo, can be divided into two main parts, articulated by a dualist relation.
In the Ginkgo project the two parts are determined by the dual condition of the context characterized by the urban environment on the east side of the site and the natural environment of the park on the west side. The term urban is associated with the term city, a product made by man, opposed to nature. The building is also formed by two parts that enter into dialogue with the character of both sides. The two

parts of the building have a dualist relation of opposites. One part is perceived as massive and the other one as lighter, one is opaque and the other one transparent, the colour of one part is dark and the other light, the texture of one part is rough and the other smooth, the light on one part reflects and on the other part doesn't.
This dualist relation expresses the eternal binary opposition that has been preserved in metaphysical and philosophical duality discourse. Following that, the parts experiment with what we could call a Cartesian dualism based on representational opposites such as body and mind, materiality and virtuality.

By contrast, the two main parts of the Black & White building are not related by opposition, but they play complementary roles. The two parts are the outer skin of the building, which has been visually characterized by its black colour, and the interior volume enclosed by the skin, which is distinguished by the white colour. The differentiation of the skin from the interior space responds to the necessity of creating an independent interface that visually articulates the relation between the building and its context and, at the same time, the relation between the interior space and the exterior views. The perforations of different sizes in the black skin minimize the exterior appearance of the building in relation to the context and at the same time these perforations, which seem to be randomly arranged in the facade, create openings of different dimensions and sizes inside the rooms. Each apartment enjoys different sizes and distribution of openings and therefore each one establishes a specific relation with the exterior space, by framing the views in a different way.
The apparent free position and size of windows in the facade responds to an invisible set of functional demands such as the positioning of floors and walls behind the facade, the necessity of natural light depending on the size of the rooms that dictates the size of each window, and the interior layout of the rooms and the possibility or impossibility of creating windows down to its floor. The final design of the outer skin is the result of overlaying all these interior and exterior demands, resulting in a complex entity that deals with many different layers in an articulated perception.

4 Scale, repetition and difference: Post-Fordist perception

The repetition of architectural elements has been a constant parameter in architectural history. The first funerary monuments were based on the geometrical disposition of vertical stones. The repetition of identical columns created the peristyle of the Greek temples, and the repetition of windows, columns, niches and arches have marked the image of classical architecture.

But the relationship between repetition and difference has changed over history in tandem with the evolution of production systems and, by extension, with the organization of labour. The process of standardization developed in the manufacturing systems initiated during the industrial revolution in Europe, resulted in the Fordist production based on the revolutionary ideas of the assembly line developed by Henry Ford to produce the Ford T, in which the cost of each piece dropped considerably thanks to the massive production of only one single model. Fordism influenced the architecture of the 20th century by making the repetition of identical pieces a symbol not only of productive efficiency but also of modernity.

The later development of information technology and its application in robotization allowed industry to improve efficiency and, at the same time, to create a wide variety of products that are not necessarily equal. Post-Fordist production not only influenced the way we conceive society, proceeding parallel to the individualization phenomenon described by Ulrich Beck and Zygmunt Bauman, but also influenced our understanding of architecture. The relation between repetition and difference in architecture is no longer seen as the consequence and result of economic and productive efficiency. Nowadays, other cultural layers play a role defining current architecture and its perception. The repetition of identical pieces is no longer a symbol of progress. Instead, difference has become a symbol of our times, a symbol of the expression of the diversity that characterizes current society.

If we assume that a relationship exists between production, society, architecture and perception created by architecture, we can formulate that Fordist society is linked to a Fordist perception and our current Post-Fordist society is linked to Post-Fordist perception. While Fordist perception was limited by visual repetition with no difference of many identical elements, Post-Fordist perception is born from experimentation with combinatorial strategies that minimize repetition and maximize visual diversity.

The Black & White building rejects the idea of repeating the same window type and size throughout the whole facade of the building, something associated with 'Fordist perception'. Not only because, in terms of production cost, the repetition of identical industrialized elements does not have as much impact as it did in the past, but also because it does not represent the cultural and social context of today, which contrasts with the context in the past in which the efficient and economical yet also massive and monotonous structures of the post-war period represented an alienated society with no space for individual differentiation.

Although the use of difference in terms of type, size and position of windows expresses individuality and diversity, the Black & White building also emphasizes its collective character. There is a certain level of repetition of window type and size, and position of distinctive elements that creates rhythm and balance in the perception of the building. Indeed, scale plays an important role in creating diversity with a certain level of uniformity. For instance, the fact that all the windows of the building have square proportions, independently of their size, makes it possible to create a strong visual relation among them, following the gestalt principle of invariance that states that simple geometrical objects are recognized independently of transformations in scale.

Due to the fact that the exterior design of the building has a direct impact in its interior, the rhythmical image of the exterior produces differences among housing types. The rational layout based on the repetition of four similar apartments on each level in an antisymmetric composition is transformed by the alternating position of the double-height voids created between the first and second floors and the second and third floors. The differentiation among the apartments is generated by a clear logical system that links the typological variety to the exterior dynamic perception of the building, resulting in a catalogue of housing types that promotes variety with a certain level of repetition.

The printed glazed skin of the Ginkgo project has been designed by experimenting with the repetition and difference among the vegetal motives printed on the glass to create a virtual green facade. The Ginkgo project rejects the solution of repeating one unique print along the whole glass facade. First, because by experimenting with a large catalogue of different printed panels and a complex combinatory strategy to arrange them in different ways, we can control the visual perception to the point that repetition is no longer perceived and therefore the parts are not distinguished within the whole. The whole design then appears to the observer as randomly generated and related to the logic of nature. Second, because current technology provides the opportunity to customize the production of these panels to the point that each one can be totally different, with little effect on the production time and cost. And third, because repetition still represents mechanization, and difference represents nature and craftmanship. A craftsmanlike way of thinking that is paradoxically produced in our Post-Fordist society with sophisticated industrial technology.

5 The talking skin: symbolic perception

The human being has decorated his skin since time immemorial. Every civilization has cultivated different sophisticated ways to change the appearance of the body. The different techniques of making up have become an intrinsic part of human civilizations, and among them the tattoo could be considered one of the most elaborate. The social connotations of the decoration of the human skin in different cultures have been analyzed in numerous studies by Claude Lévi-Strauss, such as the facial painting of the Caduveo tribe of Brazil or the Maori tattoo in New Zealand. Many anthropologists and ethnographers have examined the role of the skin as a communication device and as an interface between the one and the others.

In architecture, the skin of buildings has acquired a new and prominent role in recent years. The skin of buildings has reached a high level of autonomy, not only technical, but also semantic, and it has become an important element of the symbolic perception of architecture. This autonomy has been the subject of experimentation in both projects, Black & White and Ginkgo, thanks to the conceptual separation of their skins from the rest, concentrating on them part of the communicative function of the building.

The negotiating character of the skin of the Black & White building can be summarized by the oxymoron domestic monumentality, which like many other oxymora such as serious joke, irregular pattern or friendly fire describes complex and ambiguous phenomena created by combining two contradictory terms. The contradiction between the associated terms is provoked by the wish to achieve a compromise between the domestic interior necessities and the exterior collective expression of the building. The large scale of some facade elements such as the double height openings, which articulates the exterior perception of the architectural object, does not correspond with the necessity of smaller windows in the dwellings. The skin of the building is the element responsible for negotiating with both realities. As a result of that, the views from the inside of the building are highly articulated, creating a large variety of perceptions that relate the interior space and the exterior landscape.

In contrast, the vegetal glazed facade of the Ginkgo project works as a visual oxymoron created by the paradoxical relation between the object and its materialization as exemplified by the ones artificial grass, electric candles or invisible ink. Such contradictory associations can be only understood as the necessity today to respond to new social demands with new means of visual expression. The social demand to create affordable housing that can be met with dense construction confronts the demand in small villages to protect their visual appearance.

Many times the contradictory contemporary demands can only be solved with contemporary architectural mechanisms that make architecture disappear. In 1980 Paul Virilio stated in his book The Aesthetics of Disappearance that 'after the age of architecture-sculpture we are now in the time of cinematographic fictitiousness; literally as well as figuratively, from now on architecture is only a movie'. Almost thirty years later Kengo Kuma declared in his book Anti-Object: The Dissolution and Disintegration of Architecture that his ultimate aim was to 'erase' architecture. The architecture of disappearance has sense if we interpret the term disappearance not as absence of materiality, but as a lack of visual appearance or at least as an ambiguous appearance. Contemporary mechanisms to dissolve, disintegrate, fade out and camouflage architecture constantly play with the capacity of the skin of the building to produce an ambiguous perception in the observer.

The particular properties of glass such as transparency, translucency and reflection allow glazed facades in combination with natural and artificial light to play an effective role in creating invisible skins capable of provoking an ambiguous perception of the building. Sometimes this ambiguous perception results when the perception of the building melts with the perception of the reflection of the surroundings on its glazed facade; at other times it results when the incidence of natural light on the translucent facade produces the optical dissolution of the contour of the building.

In that sense, the park facade of the Ginkgo project is an experiment with the perception of disappearance through the use of several levels of transparency in the glazed facade and the vegetal motives printed on it. The reflection on the glass of the abundant nature around the building merges with the printed vegetation on the glass. The talking skin works as a device that confuses our senses, minimizes the physical presence of the building and renders the comprehension of its ambiguous image more difficult.

The hyperrealist vegetal images printed on the glazed facade of the Ginkgo building work as a visual oxymoron, which has been successfully accepted by inhabitants and neighbours. But as happens to many other visual oxymora, its success depends on its contradictory and paradoxical nature, which is strongly linked to our 'liquid modernity', as Bauman put it. The Ginkgo virtual glazed facade encapsulates the spirit of our times, like a pierced body or a tattooed skin.

Perception has also been used as a tool to blur the physical limit of the park houses of the Ginkgo project, which are fully integrated into the public park without any visual sign as a fence or wall to demarcate the limit between public and private property. The invisible fence allows the interior of the house and the park to connect visually and at the same time indicates the property limit with a green slope that creates a level difference that provides privacy for the inhabitants of the houses. Perception codes have been reversed and the visual stimulus produced by a common fence has been substituted in this case by another stimulus that affects the kinaesthetic sense produced by the incline of the slope, making our movement more difficult when we approach the private property.

Rethinking phenomenological architecture in the global age

We live in a global age, and following many sociologists such as Zygmunt Bauman, globalization has reached a point of no return. In the last century globalization experimented with the rise of what Émile Durkheim called mass society. At the end of the 20th century, a number of major social, technological, cultural and economic transformations converged to give rise to a new form of society, which authors such as Manuel Castells and Jan Van Dijk called the Network Society. During this social evolution the multisensory experience that provides the direct perception of reality has been deeply transformed thanks first to the impact of mass media, and more recently due to the development of new communication technologies. In the last century, the birth of the cinema reduced to two dimensions and two senses the experience of reality. Today, many people do not mind — indeed, they even prefer — to follow sports events, concerts and religious ceremonies on television at home, missing the three-dimensional experience of the stadium, the special resonance of the music in the opera house, and the smell of incense floating in the dense air of a Gothic cathedral. Network society has changed not only the way we communicate, but also our sensory experience when we communicate, which has progressively deteriorated with the development of new communication technologies. The five senses involved in a face-to-face conversation have been reduced to just sounds of a telephone conversation, a few short sentences in an SMS, and now to just 140 characters in a tweet.

Yet while we communicate in shorter and quicker spaces, we communicate more and with more people. A growing number of social activities, which were previously developed in the real world, are today developed in the virtual world. While in many aspects of our lives virtuality is gaining ground on reality, the wider concept of multisensory perception is declining in importance in favour of concepts such as convenience or productivity. Consumer society promotes the idea that new technological commodities are indispensable for life, while other aspects of our lives are superfluous and are things that everybody could ignore for the sake of progress. In this context, extremely flat culture communicates more and better because there is no time to lose. The communication rules of the network society are reducing architecture to just an image. And in fact architecture is often designed today as an image, thereby losing the possible multiple layers of perception.

But how can perception again play an important role in the architecture of the Network Society? How can subjectivity get acquire in an increasingly objectively orientated society? How can a phenomenological architecture that promotes the link between architecture and place coexist with the reality of globalization?

Revisiting phenomenological architecture in our current society is an important task in trying to maximize the multisensory perception of our environment. But, even more importantly, rethinking phenomenological architecture in a global age should also be orientated to play a functional role in the construction of our future cities. A reloaded phenomenological architecture can play an important role in facing the challenges of the current and future process of urbanization on the planet, such as densification, environmental sustainability and social identity. Architecture, after all, must create better cities, a better society and a better world.

Biographies

Helena Casanova / Jesus Hernandez

Helena Casanova

1967	born in Madrid
1997	degree in architecture from ETSAM Faculty of Architecture, Madrid
1999–2000	works at West 8, Rotterdam
2000–2001	works at Neutelings Riedijk architecten, Rotterdam
2001	founds Casanova + Hernandez Architects, Rotterdam
2009–	commission member of the Stimuleringsfonds Creatieve Industrie
2002–2013	teaches at Berlage Institute, Rotterdam; Shenzhen University, Shenzen; American University, Beirut; TU Delft; Chalmers University of Architecture, Göteborg

Jesus Hernandez

1967	born in Madrid
1997	degree in architecture, urban planning and landscape architecture from ETSAM Faculty of Architecture, Madrid
1999–2000	works at West 8, Rotterdam
2000–2001	works at Claus en Kaan architecten, Rotterdam
2001	founds Casanova + Hernandez Architects, Rotterdam
2009–	member of Spanish Association of Landscape Architects
2002–2013	teaches at Berlage Institute, Rotterdam; Shenzhen University, Shenzen; American University, Beirut; TU Delft; Chalmers University of Architecture, Göteborg

Casanova + Hernandez Architects

2013	Ceramic Museum and Park, Jinzhou
2012	*Europan 6* housing / healthcare center, Groningen
	Black and White Twins housing, Blaricum
2011	*The Ginkgo Project* housing, Beekbergen
2010	Cooltower, Rotterdam, competition First Prize
	Care-housing, Blaricum, competition First Prize
2009	*Green Window* public space, Lausanne
2005	Patio-dwellings, Groningen
2003	Europan 7, the Hague, competition First Prize
2001–	lectures, exhibitions, juries for architecture competitions in Europe, US and Asia

Claus Käpplinger

1963	born in Alzey
1985 – 1990	studies of social and art history, philosophy and sociology in Mainz, Perugia and Berlin
1987 – 1990	guest-student of the Faculty of Architecture at Technical University Berlin
1991	scientific collaborator of the German Architecture Museum (DAM) in Frankfurt / Main
1992 – 1997	architecture critic for Deutsche Kulturradio
1994 – 1996	initiator and organizer of the group *Berlin und seine Zeit* with 40 young German and Austrian architects
1998 –	organizer of the interdisciplinary circle *Stadtsalon* (since 2007 *BDA-Stadtsalon Berlin*) with architects, critics, researchers and administrators addressing questions concerning the city, architecture and perception
2009	deputy editor of the architectural review *Greenbuilding*

Reviews

Architektur Aktuell (Vienna), *DBZ Deutsche Bauzeitschrift* (Gütersloh), *Oris* (Zagreb), *De Architect* (The Hague)

Teaching

Technical University Berlin, University of the Arts Berlin, University of Applied Sciences Detmold, Nagoya City University, Technical University Brunswick

Selected Publications

Deutschland und das System Star, in DAM: Ready for Take Off, Frankfurt 2008
Grüntuch Ernst Architekten: Urban Upgrade, Aedes, Berlin 2006
Brunnert + Partner: rethinking airports, Aedes, Berlin 2004
Titus Bernhard Architekten: 9 x 9 Sinnlicher Minimalismus, Aedes, Berlin 2004
Barkow Leibinger Architekten: Cultivating the landscape, Aedes, Berlin 1999
Young French Architects, Birkhäuser, Basel-Berlin-New York 1999
Hansen + Petersen, Birkhäuser, Basel-Berlin-New York 1998
ST raum a.: in[between], Aedes, Berlin 1997
Dictionnaire de l´Architecture du XXe siècle, ed. Hazan, Paris 1996 – (the German section)
Future Housing, Institut für Auslandsbeziehungen, Tübingen 1996

Ulrich Müller

1965	born in Merseburg
1986 – 1993	studies of architecture in Weimar and Darmstadt
1993 – 2002	works a an architect in Berlin
1999	founds Architektur Galerie Berlin
since 2001	publisher of exhibitions catalogues
	in addition to lecturing on architectural communication
2009 –	publisher of AAB – Architektur Ausstellungen Berlin
2012	founds online platform AAD – Architektur Ausstellungen Deutschland

Solo exhibitions in Architektur Galerie Berlin

AFF, AllesWirdGut, Anderhalten, ARTEC, Behles & Jochimsen, Caramel, Fuhrimann Hächler, Tatiana Bilbao, Christ & Gantenbein, Holzer Kobler, E2A, EM2N, Gigon / Guyer, kadawittfeld, Adolf Krischanitz, Peter Märkli, Modersohn & Freiesleben, Riegler Riewe, Schneider + Schumacher, Simon Ungers

Curator of group exhibitions

Architektur + Fotografie ² (Iwan Baan / Hertha Hurnaus / Jan Bitter), 2012
Architektur + Fotografie (Hélène Binet / Friederike von Rauch / Christian Richters), 2011
Temporäre Kunsthalle Berlin, 2008
Architektur + Kunst – Dialoge (Max Dudler / Adolf Krischanitz / Peter Märkli), 2005
Architektur Landschaft Fotografie (Helfenstein / Müller / Ott / Schink / Spiluttini / Walti), 1999

Publications

Roger Boltshauser – Transformator, Wasmuth Verlag, Tübingen Berlin 2012
Kleihues + Kleihues – Kunst an Architektur, Wasmuth Verlag, Tübingen Berlin 2010
Architektur Galerie Berlin. Einführungen 2006 – 2009, Wasmuth Verlag, Tübingen Berlin 2009
Uwe Schröder – Bauwerk, Gebr. Mann Verlag, Berlin 2007
Architektur + Kunst – Dialoge, Gebr. Mann Verlag, Berlin 2005
Architektur Landschaft Fotografie, Gebr. Mann Verlag, Berlin 2001
Stadt Haus Architektur, Gebr. Mann Verlag, Berlin 2000

Project information

The Black and White Twins

Address	Cederplein 1-27 1261 ZV Blaricum, The Netherlands
Program	Housing
Architect	Casanova + Hernandez Architects Pannekoekstraat 104, 3011 LL Rotterdam, The Netherlands www.casanova-hernandez.com
Client	Blauwhoed Eurowoningen
Construction	2012
Cost	2.7 Mio. Euro (excl. VAT)

The Ginkgo Project

Address	Koningspage 1-7 7361 ZR Beekbergen, The Netherlands
Program	Housing
Architect	Casanova + Hernandez Architects Pannekoekstraat 104, 3011 LL Rotterdam, The Netherlands www.casanova-hernandez.com
Client	Sprengenland Wonen
Construction	2011
Cost	3.6 Mio. Euro (excl. VAT)

The book is published on the occasion of the exhibition
Casanova + Hernandez *Scale & Perception*
Architektur Galerie Berlin
May 17 – June 29, 2013

Editor: Ulrich Müller
Architektur Galerie Berlin   Karl-Marx-Allee 96   10243 Berlin, Germany
www.architekturgalerieberlin.de

Concept and layout: Ulrich Müller with Casanova + Hernandez
Images: Christian Richters, Casanova + Hernandez (p. 27, 28, 29, 55, 59)
Drawings: Casanova + Hernandez Architects

A CIP catalogue record for this book is available from the German National Library
Production: Medialis Offsetdruck, Berlin

Exclusive distributor: Ernst Wasmuth Verlag Tübingen • Berlin
www.wasmuth-verlag.de

Printed in Germany
ISBN 978 3 8030 0766 7

With kind support from

creative industries fund NL   BARTELS   PVBmotiv   REYNAERS   ROVAL   sprengenland wonen